T0001271

Best Easy Day Hikes
Jacksonville, Florida

Help Us Keep This Guide Up to Date

Every effort has been made by the author and editors to make this guide as accurate and useful as possible. However, many things can change after a guide is published—regulations change, facilities come under new management, and so forth.

We would love to hear from you concerning your experiences with this guide and how you feel it could be improved and kept up to date. While we may not be able to respond to all comments and suggestions, we'll take them to heart, and we'll also make certain to share them with the author. Please send your comments and suggestions to falconeditorial@rowman.com.

Thanks for your input!

Best Easy Day Hikes Series

Best Easy Day Hikes
Jacksonville, Florida

Second Edition

Johnny Molloy

FALCONGUIDES

ESSEX, CONNECTICUT

FALCONGUIDES®

An imprint of Globe Pequot, the trade division of
The Rowman & Littlefield Publishing Group, Inc.
4501 Forbes Blvd., Ste. 200
Lanham, MD 20706
www.rowman.com

Falcon and FalconGuides are registered trademarks and Make Adventure Your Story is a trademark of The Rowman & Littlefield Publishing Group, Inc.

Distributed by NATIONAL BOOK NETWORK

Copyright © 2024 The Rowman & Littlefield Publishing Group, Inc.

Maps by The Rowman & Littlefield Publishing Group, Inc.

All rights reserved. No part of this book may be reproduced in any form or by any electronic or mechanical means, including information storage and retrieval systems, without written permission from the publisher, except by a reviewer who may quote passages in a review.

British Library Cataloguing in Publication Information available

Library of Congress Cataloging-in-Publication Data

Names: Molloy, Johnny, 1961– author.
Title: Best easy day hikes Jacksonville, Florida / Johnny Molloy.
Description: Second edition. | Essex, Connecticut : Falcon Guides, [2024] | Series: Falconguides | "Maps by The Rowman & Littlefield Publishing Group, Inc."—t.p. verso.
Identifiers: LCCN 2023052340 (print) | LCCN 2023052341 (ebook) | ISBN 9781493079001 (paper : acid-free paper) | ISBN 9781493079018 (electronic)
Subjects: LCSH: Day hiking—Florida—Jacksonville—Guidebooks. | Hiking—Florida—Jacksonville—Guidebooks. | Walking—Florida—Jacksonville—Guidebooks. | Trails—Florida—Jacksonville—Guidebooks. | Jacksonville (Fla.)—Guidebooks.
Classification: LCC GV199.42.F62 J335 2024 (print) | LCC GV199.42.F62 (ebook) | DDC 796.5109759/12—dc23/eng/20231227
LC record available at https://lccn.loc.gov/2023052340
LC ebook record available at https://lccn.loc.gov/2023052341

♾️™ The paper used in this publication meets the minimum requirements of American National Standard for Information Sciences—Permanence of Paper for Printed Library Materials, ANSI/NISO Z39.48-1992.

The author and The Rowman & Littlefield Publishing Group, Inc., assume no liability for accidents happening to, or injuries sustained by, readers who engage in the activities described in this book.

Contents

The Hikes

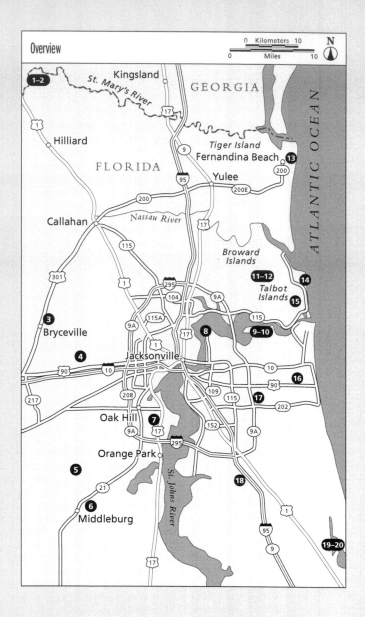

Acknowledgments

Thanks to all the people who helped me with this book, primarily all the staff at Falcon. Also, thanks to all the park personnel who tirelessly answered my questions while trying to manage these jewels of the First Coast. The biggest thanks go to the trail builders and hikers of the greater Jacksonville area; without y'all, the trails wouldn't be there in the first place.

About the Author

Johnny Molloy is a full-time writer and adventurer and Christian. Cutting his teeth in the Great Smoky Mountains, Johnny became skilled in a variety of outdoor environments, sharing his love of the great outdoors while writing more than eighty-five books, including hiking, camping, and paddling guides covering twenty-eight states. Molloy has also written numerous articles for magazines, websites, and blogs. He resides in Johnson City, Tennessee, but spends his winters hiking, paddling, and camping all over Florida. For the latest on Molloy's pursuits and work, please visit www .johnnymolloy.com.

Introduction

The boardwalk extends beyond the shore over the St. Johns River. Sitting on a bench, I look westward across the water, toward downtown. The mighty river—the flowing pulse of Jacksonville, with its freshwater tributaries extending inland and tidal tentacles meeting the Atlantic Ocean—flows past the location of many hikes in this book. My mind soars beyond downtown while mentally recounting all the scenic hikes of greater Jacksonville.

To the east, maritime hammock woods, vast shell mounds, and river views await hikers at Fort Caroline. The protected area of the Talbot Islands contains several trails that wander over ancient wooded dunes, astride tidal creeks bordered by marsh grasses, and even along the Atlantic Ocean. To the north, the green oasis of the Ralph E. Simmons State Forest protects the woods and paths running beside the St. Mary's River, a magnificent blackwater stream that originates in the Okefenokee Swamp and flows to the sea, where the trails and history of Fort Clinch State Park await hikers.

To the south stands the jewel of Castaway Island Preserve, where boardwalks and nature trails allow hikers to explore a slice of coastal Duval County near popular beaches. Beyond that, the protected woodlands at the University of North Florida offer a five century-old bald cypress tree, scenic lakes, and a multiplicity of Florida plant and animal communities. The gorgeous waters and woods of the GTM Reserve harbor marine, avian, and land wildlife. To the west, across the St. Johns River, Cary State Forest features a loop trail that cuts into the heart of a swamp hammock, where wetland woodlands regally rise to the sky, encircled by towering pines, with the promise of more trails in the future. The Black

Creek Ravines, a conservation project initiated by the St. Johns Water Management District, includes paths that lace its sandhills, richly vegetated ravines, and Black Creek itself. Interpretive information, dark, mysterious creeks, and an ever-changing Florida mosaic of eye-appealing scenery are all part of the trail experience at the vast Jennings State Forest.

With this book in hand and willing feet, you can explore these jewels of the greater Jacksonville region. No matter where you go, the trails in this book will enhance your outdoor experience and leave you with an appreciation of the natural splendors of the First Coast. Enjoy!

The Nature of Greater Jacksonville

Jacksonville's hiking grounds range from single-track wooded trails along wild streams and salt water to flat and paved park strolls. Hikes in this guide cover the gamut. While by definition a "best easy day hike" is not strenuous and generally poses little danger to the traveler, knowing a few details about the nature of greater Jacksonville will enhance your explorations.

Weather

The climate here is Florida's most temperate, with four distinct seasons. During the long summer, highs regularly reach the 90s and a thunderstorm will come most any afternoon. Warm nights stay up in the 70s. Fall brings cooler nights and warm days with less precipitation than summer, and marks the beginning of the hiking season. Winter is variable: Highs push 65 degrees, but expect lows in the 40s, though sub-freezing temperatures are the norm during cold snaps. There are usually several mild days during each winter month.

Precipitation comes in strong continental fronts, with persistent rains followed by sunny, cold days. The longer days of spring begin the warm-up process, even becoming hot, but temperatures can vary wildly. Heat returns with summer, curtailing the hiking season.

Critters

Jacksonville trail treaders will encounter mostly benign creatures on these trails, such as deer, armadillos, squirrels, rabbits, wild turkeys, and even bears are a possibility. A variety of songbirds on land complement shorebirds abounding on Jacksonville's waters. More rarely seen (during the daylight hours especially) are coyotes, raccoons, and opossums. Deer in some of the parks are remarkably tame and may linger on or close to the trail as you approach. Alligators may be present near water. If you feel uncomfortable when encountering any critter, keep your distance, and they will generally keep theirs.

Be Prepared

Hiking in greater Jacksonville is generally safe. Still, hikers should be prepared, whether they are out for a short stroll at Blue Cypress Park or venturing into the secluded Ralph E. Simmons State Forest. Some specific advice:

- Know the basics of first aid, including how to treat bleeding, bites and stings, and fractures, strains, or sprains. Pack a first-aid kit on each excursion.
- Familiarize yourself with the symptoms of heat exhaustion and heat stroke. Heat exhaustion symptoms include heavy sweating, muscle cramps, headache, dizziness, and fainting. Should you or any of your hiking party exhibit any of these symptoms, cool the victim down

immediately by rehydrating and getting them to an air-conditioned location. Cold showers also help reduce body temperature. Heat stroke is much more serious: The victim's skin is hot and dry to the touch, and they may lose consciousness. In this event, call 911 immediately.

- Regardless of the weather, your body needs a lot of water while hiking. A full 32-ounce bottle is the minimum for these short hikes, but more is always better. Bring a full water bottle, whether water is available along the trail or not.
- Don't drink from streams, rivers, creeks, or lakes without treating or filtering the water first. Waterways and water bodies may host a variety of contaminants, including giardia, which can cause serious intestinal unrest.
- Prepare for extremes of both heat and cold by dressing in layers.
- Carry a backpack in which you can store extra clothing, ample drinking water and food, and whatever goodies you might want, like guidebooks, cameras, and binoculars. Consider bringing a GPS with tracking capabilities.
- Almost all Jacksonville trails have cell-phone coverage. Bring your device, but make sure you've turned it off, or keep it on the vibrate setting while hiking. Nothing like a "wake the dead" ring to startle every creature, including fellow hikers.
- Keep children under careful watch. Trails travel along many rivers, streams, lakes, and the ocean, none of which are recommended for swimming. Hazards along some of the trails include poison ivy, uneven footing, and steep

drop-offs, so make sure children don't stray from the designated route. Children should carry a plastic whistle; if they become lost, they should stay in one place and blow the whistle to summon help.

Zero Impact

Trails in Jacksonville and neighboring communities are well used year-round, save for the dog days of summer. As trail users, we must be especially vigilant to make sure our passage leaves no lasting mark. Here are some basic guidelines for preserving trails in the region:

- Pack out all your own trash, including biodegradable items such as orange peels. You might also pack out garbage left by less-considerate hikers.
- Don't approach or feed any wild creatures—the ground squirrel eyeing your snack food is best able to survive if it remains self-reliant.
- Don't pick wildflowers or gather rocks, antlers, feathers, and other treasures along the trail. Removing these items will only take away from the next hiker's experience.
- Avoid damaging trailside soils and plants by remaining on the established route. This is also a good rule of thumb for avoiding poison ivy and other common regional trailside irritants.
- Be courteous by not making loud noises while hiking.
- Many of these trails are multiuse, which means you'll share them with other hikers, trail runners, mountain bikers, and equestrians. Familiarize yourself with the proper trail etiquette, yielding the trail when appropriate.
- Use outhouses at trailheads or along the trail.

Jacksonville Area Boundaries and Corridors

For the purposes of this guide, best easy day hikes are confined to a 1-hour drive from downtown Jacksonville and are primarily in Duval County. Other hikes reach into the counties of Nassau and Clay.

A number of major highways and interstates converge in Jacksonville. Directions to trailheads are given from these arteries. They include I-95, I-295, and SR 9A—the east side of the interstate loop around Jacksonville.

Land Management

The following government organizations manage most of the public lands described in this guide and can provide further information on these hikes and other trails in their service areas.

- Florida State Parks, Florida Department of Environmental Protection, Division of Recreation and Parks, 3900 Commonwealth Blvd., MS 535, Tallahassee, FL 32399; (850) 245-2157; www.FloridaStateParks.org
- Florida Division of Forestry, 3125 Conner Blvd., Tallahassee, FL 32399-1650; (850) 681-5800; www.fdacs.gov
- Jacksonville Parks & Recreation, 7000 Roosevelt Blvd., Jacksonville, FL 32244; (904) 255-7919; www.jaxparks.com
- St. Johns Water Management District, 7775 Baymeadows Way, Ste. 102, Jacksonville, FL 32256; (904) 730-6270; www.sjrwmd.com
- Timucuan Ecological and Historic Preserve, 12713 Fort Caroline Rd., Jacksonville, FL 32225; (904) 641-7155; www.nps.gov/timu

How to Use This Guide

This guide is designed to be simple and easy to use. Each hike is described with a map and summary information that delivers the trail's vital statistics, including length, difficulty, fees and permits, park hours, canine compatibility, and trail contacts. Directions to the trailhead are also provided, along with a general description of what you'll see along the way. A detailed route finder (Miles and Directions) sets forth mileages between significant landmarks along the trail.

Hike Selection

This guide describes trails that are accessible to every hiker, whether visiting from out of town or someone lucky enough to live in greater Jacksonville. The hikes are no longer than 7 miles round-trip, and most are considerably shorter. They range in difficulty from flat excursions perfect for a family outing to more challenging hilly treks. While these trails are among the best, keep in mind that nearby trails, often in the same park or preserve, may offer options better suited to your needs. I've sought to space hikes throughout the greater Jacksonville region, so wherever your starting point, you'll find a great easy day hike nearby.

Difficulty Ratings

These are all easy hikes, but *easy* is a relative term. To aid in the selection of a hike that suits particular needs and abilities, each is rated easy, moderate, or more challenging. Bear in mind that even the more challenging routes can be made easy by hiking within your limits and taking rests when you need them.

- **Easy** hikes are generally short and flat, taking no longer than 1 hour to complete.
- **Moderate** hikes involve increased distance and relatively mild changes in elevation, and will take 1 to 2 hours to complete.
- **More challenging** hikes feature some steep stretches, greater distances, and generally take longer than 2 hours to complete.

These are completely subjective ratings; consider that what you think is easy is entirely dependent on your level of fitness and the adequacy of your gear (primarily shoes). If you are hiking with a group, you should select a hike with a rating that's appropriate for the least-fit and -prepared person in your party.

Approximate hiking times assume that on flat ground, most walkers average 2 miles per hour. Adjust that rate according to the steepness of the terrain and your level of fitness (subtract time if you're an aerobic animal, and add time if you're hiking with kids), and you'll have a ballpark hiking duration. Be sure to add more time if you plan to picnic or take part in other activities, like bird-watching or photography.

Trail Finder

Best Hikes for River and Stream Lovers

Best Hikes for Children

Best Hikes for Dogs

Best Hikes for Great Views

Best Hikes for Boardwalks

Best Hikes for History Buffs

Best Hikes for Nature Lovers

Map Legend

≡95≡	Interstate Highway
─{301}─	U.S. Highway
─(10)─	State Highway
───────	Local Road
= = = = =	Unpaved Road
▬▬▬▬▬	Featured Trail
- - - - - -	Trail
～～～	River/Creek
⬭	Body of Water
—·—··—··	State Border
•—•—•—•	Power line
🛥	Boat Launch
⏑	Bridge
▲	Camping
▲	Camping (backcountry)
•—•	Gate
🅿	Parking
⊞	Picnic Area
■	Point of Interest/Structure
🛈	Ranger Station
🚻	Restroom
🛗	Tower
○	Town
⓫	Trailhead
🖼	Viewpoint/Overlook
❓	Visitor Center

1   White Sand Landing Loop

This lengthy trek travels the heart of Ralph E. Simmons State Forest, making a side trip to pretty White Sand Landing, on the banks of the scenic St. Mary's River. Leave the river, passing through myriad natural communities, which increase your chances for seeing wildlife. Backpackers take note that two backcountry campsites lie along the route.

Distance: 7.2-mile loop
Approximate hiking time: 3.5 to 4 hours
Difficulty: More challenging due to distance
Trail surface: Natural surfaces
Best season: Oct through Apr
Other trail users: Equestrians
Canine compatibility: Leashed dogs permitted

Fees and permits: Day pass required
Schedule: Sunrise to sunset
Maps: Ralph E. Simmons State Forest, USGS Boulogne
Trail contacts: Ralph E. Simmons State Forest, 3742 Clint Dr., Hilliard, FL 32046-4905; (904) 845-4933; www.fdacs.gov

Finding the trailhead: From exit 28A, New Kings Road, on I-295 near Jacksonville, take US 1 north to Callahan. From the intersection of US 1 and SR A1A in Callahan, continue north for 17.8 miles to Lake Hampton Road, just before the US 1 bridge over the St. Mary's River. Ignore signs for Ralph E. Simmons State Forest until you reach Lake Hampton Road. Turn right on Lake Hampton Road and follow it for 2.5 miles to Penny Haddock Road. Turn left on Penny Haddock Road and follow it for 0.8 mile, then veer left into the trailhead parking area. GPS trailhead coordinates: 30.794028, -81.938444

The Hike

This is the longest hike in this guidebook. It offers a chance to not only test your physical skills but also to explore the remote heart of the Ralph E. Simmons State Forest, and perhaps to see wildlife scattered amid the numerous plant ecosystems in the St. Mary's River valley near the Georgia border. The loop, known as the White Trail, is marked with white diamond blazes as it joins and uses old forest roads. However, where these roads meet or divide, the correct route is clearly marked with the blazes, so don't be afraid of getting lost. If you go some distance without seeing a white blaze, then back up. Do expect to hear the afternoon wind pushing through the trees, and perhaps a deer rustling away in an oak thicket, or an armadillo digging at the soil.

The forest continually changes character, from open pine flatwoods to crowded swamp hardwoods, thick with ferns and cane, especially in the bottoms closer to the river. The two recommended campsites located along the St. Mary's River off the main loop are first come, first served, and are accessible only by foot or boat. The St. Mary's is a fine paddling river. Do not bypass the spur trail to White Sand Landing, a riverside beach and campsite shaded by live oaks. Somebody with a good arm—and a rock—could throw a stone to Georgia from there.

The White Trail leaves the trailhead and high ground and aims for the St. Mary's River. It comes within 0.25 mile of the river and then turns north and runs roughly parallel with the St. Mary's. You can see the river before angling south back toward the trailhead. In most places swamp woods divide the trail from the river. An aura of seclusion accompanies you throughout the hike. Hunting is allowed in the state forest, so make sure and check ahead of time for hunt dates at http://myfwc.com.

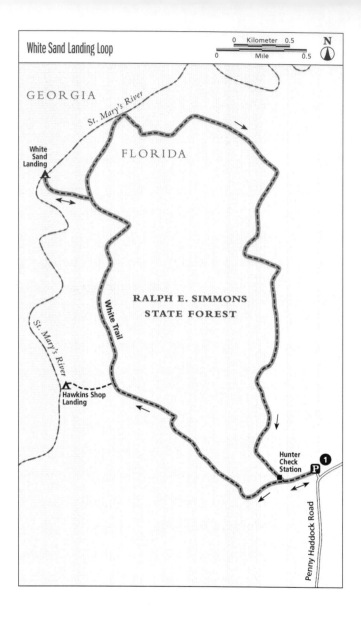

Miles and Directions

0.0 Pass around a gate near the trailhead kiosk, traveling westerly on a double-track of sand and plant fodder. Turkey oaks and pine shade the path.

0.1 Reach a hunter check station. Here the path divides. Stay left with the white blazes, now on a narrower track.

0.4 Reach a sand fire road junction in longleaf pines. Stay right with white blazes, heading northwesterly.

1.0 Stay left at an intersection, downhill into moist woodland.

1.5 A spur trail leads left to Hawkins Shop Landing Campsite, the first of two on the St. Mary's River. The spur trail is marked with a small blue sign with a tent symbol on it. The White Trail passes through row-cropped pines.

1.6 Bridge a swamp stream strand by culvert. Note the tupelo and cypress trees growing in the streambed.

2.4 Reach a "T" intersection. Here, the White Trail turns left with the white blazes and heads almost due west.

2.7 An elevated spur trail leads left through swamp hardwoods to White Sand Landing and a campsite. Take this spur trail and the opportunity to see the scenic St. Mary's River.

3.0 Make White Sand Landing. Live oaks tower over a flat sloping to a sand beach and an exemplary blackwater river.

3.3 Head north on the White Trail in lush woods after returning from White Sand Landing.

3.8 The White Trail comes within sight of open water on the St. Mary's, then turns away on a relatively faint track.

4.3 Watch for an unexpected left turn marked with white blazes. Bisect a hardwood swamp of red maple, tupelo, and widely buttressed pines.

4.7 The White Trail crosses a closed forest road. Keep straight.

5.0 Reach a "T" intersection. Stay right with the White Trail.

5.5 Head left, easterly, on an elevated road berm through seasonally inundated forest.

5.8 Head right at a trail junction, now walking southbound.

6.4 Turn left at an intersection to bridge a streamlet. Ascend on a gullied track into row-cropped pines.

6.9 Reach a major double-track sand road. Turn left toward the hunter check station.

7.1 Reach the hunter check station. Begin backtracking.

7.2 Arrive back at the trailhead.

2 St. Mary's River Trail Loop

This hike explores the Ralph E. Simmons State Forest, rolling through mixed woodland before descending to the St. Mary's River, where a sandy river access allows good views of the river dividing Florida from Georgia. Travel along the river corridor. Your return route climbs from the river bottom and then loops back to the trailhead.

Distance: 3.3-mile loop
Approximate hiking time: 1.5 to 2.5 hours
Difficulty: Moderate
Trail surface: Natural surfaces, gravel
Best season: Oct through Apr
Other trail users: Equestrians
Canine compatibility: Leashed dogs permitted

Fees and permits: Day pass required
Schedule: Sunrise to sunset
Maps: Ralph E. Simmons State Forest, USGS Boulogne
Trail contacts: Ralph E. Simmons State Forest, 3742 Clint Dr., Hilliard, FL 32046; (904) 845-4933; www.fdacs.gov

Finding the trailhead: From exit 28A, New Kings Road, on I-295 near Jacksonville, take US 1 north to Callahan. From the intersection of US 1 and SR A1A in Callahan, continue north for 17.8 miles to Lake Hampton Road, just before the US 1 bridge over the St. Mary's. Ignore signs for Ralph E. Simmons State Forest until you reach Lake Hampton Road. Turn right on Lake Hampton Road and follow it for 1.6 miles to the trailhead on your left, just beyond a set of power lines. GPS trailhead coordinates: 30.779778, -81.953056

The Hike

This hike travels through the southern portion of the Ralph E. Simmons State Forest, a 3,700-acre swath of land stretching along the St. Mary's River in Nassau County.

Interestingly, this forest has within its bounds the most northerly parcel of the Sunshine State. Throughout its length, the St. Mary's River forms the boundary line between Florida and Georgia. The forest is located within a northerly bend of the St. Mary's. The land was purchased using Preservation 2000 and Save Our Rivers funds. Hunting is allowed in the forest, so check http://myfwc.com for hunt dates before hitting the trail.

Using the St. Mary's River Trail, this adventure wanders through a forest mosaic that changes with the elevation and situation. One minute you will be traveling through turkey oaks and palmetto patches, and the next minute you will be underneath pine groves. Oak forest rises astride the St. Mary's. The trail itself is sometimes used as a dividing line in prescribed fire management. The result is sometimes differing types of forest habitats on either side of the trail you are following.

The route, primarily a double-track path with a natural duff and sand composition, is marked with yellow diamond blazes nailed to trees as it works downhill to the St. Mary's, where you also briefly join a power line. Even though this blackwater stream rises and lowers with the ocean tides, salt water never makes it this far upriver. Freshwater trees, primarily cypress, border the flow. At low tide small sand beaches are exposed in places along the river.

The path then travels downstream along the river corridor atop a bluff where you can look through the trees into Georgia. After offering views of the Peach State, the loop curves toward the trailhead. Pay attention as the vegetation changes with elevation, from swamp hardwoods to mixed woodland to longleaf pines with an understory of wiregrass. The remainder of the hike is an easy stroll through eye-appealing forest.

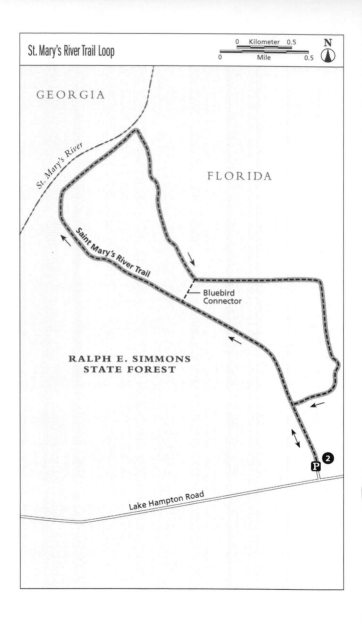

St. Mary's River Trail Loop

GEORGIA

FLORIDA

St. Mary's River

Saint Mary's River Trail

Bluebird
Connector

RALPH E. SIMMONS
STATE FOREST

P **2**

Lake Hampton Road

Miles and Directions

0.0 Leave the fenced trailhead parking area and kiosk, heading north around a road gate. Enter an area of young planted longleaf pines on the St. Mary's River Trail. Shortly join natural forest.

0.2 Reach a junction. Your return route comes in from the right. Keep straight, tracing the yellow blazes on a slight descent, shaded by laurel oak and pine.

0.8 Reach another trail junction. Here, the Bluebird Connector turns right to make a 1.8-mile loop. However, this hike keeps forward, still on the St. Mary's River Trail. The descent sharpens as you travel northwesterly for the St. Mary's River.

1.0 Reach a power line in a marshy area. The trail stays on an elevated berm under the power line.

1.3 Meet the St. Mary's River. The power line clearing affords access to the sand-bordered waterway. The St. Mary's River Trail leaves the power lines and turns northeast, roughly paralleling the St. Mary's River in dense woodland of wax myrtle, palmetto, sand live oaks, and sweetgums. Sun-exposed parts of the trail are sandy. Enjoy views from a wooded bluff.

1.6 Reach a river access, then turn away from St. Mary's, traversing a wooded wetland of tupelo and cypress.

1.7 Rise to higher ground in mixed woodland.

2.1 Level off in classic longleaf/wiregrass forest complemented with turkey oaks.

2.2 Meet the other end of the Bluebird Connector. Keep straight, still on the St. Mary's River Trail, now curving easterly through a level open forest, making for easy hiking.

2.6 The St. Mary's River Trail turns sharply right (south).

3.0 After curving west, the trail passes a St. Johns River Water Management District monitoring station.

3.1 The Yellow Trail completes its loop. Turn left here, backtracking.

3.3 Arrive back at the trailhead.

3 Cary Trailwalker Trail

This loop takes you through pine forest into the middle of a wooded swamp on an elevated boardwalk with a top-down view of wetlands. The boardwalk offers a dry-footed examination of an otherwise inaccessible ecosystem. The trek, used by school groups on field trips, then travels a grassy road to span more wetlands before returning to pine flatwoods and looping back to the trailhead.

Distance: 1.3-mile loop
Approximate hiking time: 0.5 to 1 hour
Difficulty: Easy
Trail surface: Natural surfaces, boardwalk
Best season: Oct through Apr
Other trail users: None
Canine compatibility: Leashed dogs permitted

Fees and permits: Day pass required
Schedule: Sunrise to sunset
Maps: Cary Sate Forest Recreation Map, USGS Bryceville
Trail contacts: Cary State Forest, 7465 Pavilion Dr., Bryceville, FL 32209; (904) 266-5021; www .fdacs.gov

Finding the trailhead: From exit 343 on I-10 west of downtown Jacksonville, take US 301 north for 1 mile, then veer right into the town of Baldwin on Beaver Street / US 90 / US 301. Travel for 0.6 mile east through the town, then turn left, staying with US 301, and follow it for 7.1 more miles to Pavilion Road and Cary State Forest. Turn right on Pavilion Road and follow it for 0.3 mile to the trailhead near a picnic area and kiosk at the intersection with Fire Tower Road. The trail starts on the north side of Pavilion Road. GPS trailhead coordinates: 30.400000, -81.926528

The Hike

Bring a picnic and enjoy a meal at the trailhead. You also have the option of camping here, as six campsites—enhanced with warm showers and restrooms—are located near the trailhead. Cary State Forest is located west of downtown Jacksonville near the town of Bryceville. The state forest straddles the Nassau/Duval county line. The original tract was one of the first state forests in Florida. It now has been expanded to 13,385 acres. More trails and camping opportunities are slated for the future, using the added tracts. Check the Cary State Forest website for supplemental hiking opportunities. This particular hike takes place in the westernmost part of the forest in a designated safety zone (i.e., no hunting allowed); therefore, hikers can enjoy this trail every day of the year.

The trail leaves the picnic area to enter longleaf pines with a brushy understory. The building you soon reach is the state forest teaching pavilion, used primarily for school groups. Interpretive information is scattered along the designated footpath bordered by fetterbush and yaupon, with a pine-needle and grass footbed about 5 feet wide. The natural surface soon gives way to the Adams Wilderness Boardwalk, named for the couple who donated funds to construct it. The wooden walkway allows you to enter a hardwood hammock without damaging the vegetation—or getting your feet wet and muddy.

Notice the buttressed trees. Since the moist soil can't hold these swamp trees very well, the base of their trunks and lowermost roots spread outward to keep them from tipping over. Cypress trees are easy to spot with their "knees." The function of these woody protrusions is still not known to botanists. It was once thought these knees allowed often-inundated cypresses to "breathe."

Sweetbay magnolia is another common tree in the swamp. It is a tall evergreen with a gray trunk that prefers the

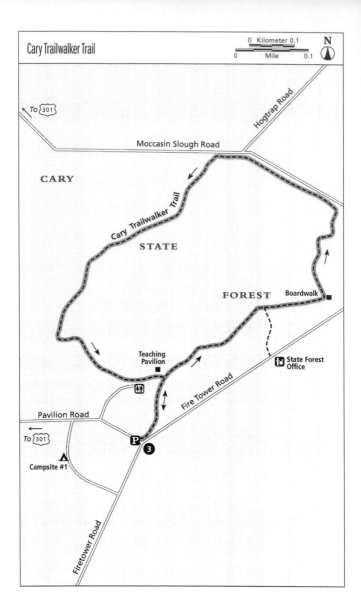

wetter margins of forests. Sweetbay's long elliptical leaves have a silvery white underside that makes it easy to identify. It is common in wetlands throughout Florida.

The boardwalk winds through the hammock, then briefly joins a sandy forest road before reentering the woods as a footpath. Meander through woodlands before returning to the teaching pavilion and restroom building.

Miles and Directions

0.0	From the trailhead kiosk walk north across Pavilion Road. Look for a sign that reads NATURE TRAIL / TEACHING PAVILION. Enter longleaf flatwoods, reaching the Teaching Pavilion, a multi-sided wood structure. Turn right here, heading northeast.
0.3	A spur path leads right toward the park office and outbuildings.
0.4	Reach a resting bench and the beginning of the boardwalk.
0.5	Leave the boardwalk to join Moccasin Slough Road, a sandy double-track closed to vehicles. Turn left here.
0.7	Hogtrap Road leaves right. The trail stays left on Moccasin Slough Road, then turns left into the woods as a footpath. Wander through pines.
1.1	Reach a "T" junction. Head left, then emerge near the restroom building. The Teaching Pavilion is within sight. Backtrack toward the picnic area and trailhead.
1.3	Arrive back at the trailhead.

4 Camp Milton Preserve Walk

Walk a series of nature trails through what was once a Confederate fort. Now you can enjoy not only the area history but also its natural beauty along McGirts Creek. It's easy to extend your hike here, as Camp Milton Preserve serves as a primary trailhead for the 14.5-mile Jacksonville-Baldwin Rail Trail.

Distance: 1.9 miles
Approximate hiking time: 1.5 to 2 hours
Difficulty: Easy
Trail surface: Poured concrete
Best season: Oct through Apr
Other trail users: None
Canine compatibility: Leashed dogs permitted

Fees and permits: No fees or permits required
Schedule: 9 a.m. to 5 p.m.
Maps: Camp Milton, USGS Marietta
Trail contacts: Camp Milton Preserve, 1225 Halsema Rd. North, Jacksonville, FL 32220; (904) 630-2489; www.JaxParks.com

Finding the trailhead: From exit 351 on I-10 west of downtown Jacksonville, take Chaffee Road north for 0.2 mile to US 90 / Beaver Road. Turn left on US 90 west / Beaver Road and follow it 1.2 miles to Halsema Road. Turn right on Halsema Road and follow it 1.5 miles to the preserve, on your right. GPS trailhead coordinates: 30.334677, -81.868629

The Hike

The Confederate Army established a fort here in 1864, trying to lure Union troops out of Jacksonville while simultaneously protecting the food pipeline running north from the cattle country of Central Florida to Rebel troops. Today, the site has not only been preserved but also enhanced with interpretive trails that explain the historic area. You can also enjoy heritage trees that are planted along the paths. These heritage trees are spliced from historic originals relevant to the Civil War. For example, a sycamore tree comes from General Robert E. Lee's family estate in Virginia. Another comes from the site of Lincoln's tomb on the Capitol Mall. Another comes from Jacksonville's very own Treaty Oak.

You can also travel over McGirts Creek on a re-created Civil War bridge. The Harvey homestead site gives you an idea of what farm life was like in the 1860s. And there is a final perk: Camp Milton Preserve is the main trailhead and midpoint for the Jacksonville-Baldwin Rail Trail. This asphalt path stretches in both directions from here, allowing you to extend your hike until your legs wear out. Or perhaps you'd prefer to hike the preserve trails and then jump on your bicycle for a ride on the rail trail. No matter how you do it, come and give this well-maintained, attractive preserve a chance.

It's hard to get up a hiking head of steam at Camp Milton because the plethora of interpretive signage is too captivating to ignore. You can always stroll around the fort preserve and then burn calories on the rail trail. From the trailhead, the Earthworks Trail will take you through open fields and into a gorgeous hardwood hammock. It then circles around earthworks left over from the fort, where 8,000 Southerners were stationed. Named for Florida governor John Milton, the fort extended beyond the boundaries of the preserve south along Halsema Road.

The hike then passes the Harvey homestead to cross the replica bridge over McGirts Creek. From there, meet the Jacksonville-Baldwin Rail Trail. Here's your opportunity to add mileage to the hike. Otherwise, backtrack toward the trailhead and pick up the American Forest Trail, where you

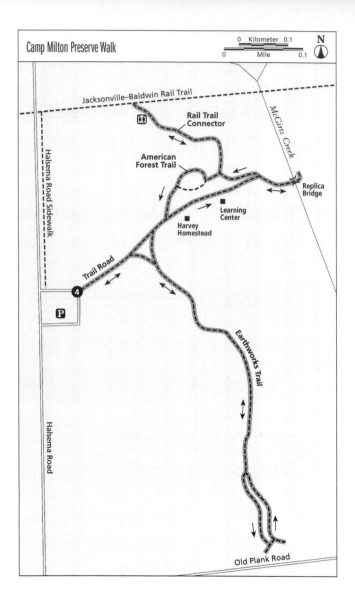

can see an abundance of heritage trees brought here from all over the South—places like the Shiloh Battlefield in Tennessee and the Andersonville Military Prison in Georgia. Learn about the Civil War while appreciating the beauty of these shade-bearing plants.

The rail trail came to be through the efforts of several government agencies. Initially, the city of Jacksonville bought the 14.5 miles of unused CSX Railroad line in 1992. Over time, the Florida Department of Greenways and Trails has gotten involved, and the trail is now an asset for Jacksonville, with Camp Milton as the centerpiece.

Miles and Directions

0.0	With your back to Halsema Road, take the double-track trail, Trail Road, lined with live oaks, easterly.
0.1	Reach a trail junction. Turn right on the Earthworks Trail. Travel through a field, then join a boardwalk through wetland woods, rife with ferns and vines.
0.4	The boardwalk splits. Begin looping around old Confederate earthworks, now thickly forested. Two boardwalk spurs extend toward Old Plank Road.
0.6	Complete the boardwalk loop and then backtrack to Trail Road.
1.0	Turn right on the Trail Road, shortly passing the Harvey homestead and the Learning Center and Historic Museum.
1.2	Cross the re-created Civil War bridge over McGirts Creek. Backtrack, then stay right, joining the Rail Trail Connector.
1.5	Meet the Jacksonville-Baldwin Rail Trail near restrooms. The asphalt track travels east-west for many a mile. This hike backtracks to pick up the American Forest Trail, then turns right to shortly reach Trail Road. Turn right on Trail Road, retracing your steps.
1.9	Arrive back at the trailhead.

5   Fire & Water Nature Trail

This hilly interpretive trail in the Jennings State Forest takes you through numerous plant communities and to informative stops that explain the importance of fire and water for Florida's forests. Enjoy a wildlife blind and an overlook above Wheeler Branch, a blackwater stream, and perhaps see some insect-eating pitcher plants.

Distance: 1.8-mile loop
Approximate hiking time: 1 to 1.5 hours
Difficulty: Moderate due to hills
Trail surface: Natural surfaces
Best season: Oct through Apr
Other trail users: None
Canine compatibility: Leashed dogs permitted

Fees and permits: Day pass required
Schedule: Sunrise to sunset
Maps: Jennings State Forest Trailwalker Trails, USGS Fiftone
Trail contacts: Jennings State Forest, 1337 Long Horn Rd., Middleburg, FL 32068; (904) 291-5330; www.fdacs.gov

---

Finding the trailhead: From exit 12 on I-295 southwest of downtown, take Blanding Boulevard (SR 21) south for 8 miles to Old Jennings Road. Turn right onto Old Jennings Road and follow it for 4.1 miles nearly to a dead end, then turn right on Live Oak Road, a sand road. Follow it for 1.5 miles to reach the trailhead on your left (at 0.5 mile, you will pass the Old Jennings Recreation Area trailhead). GPS trailhead coordinates: 30.136461, -81.882131

The Hike

Jennings State Forest stretches across 23,000 acres of fast-growing northern Clay County as well as a portion of Duval County, near the town of Middleburg. Centered on North Fork Black Creek, the forest provides recreational opportunities for visitors and a place for wildlife to call home. Land managers are anxious to restore this area to preserve the natural communities vital to northeast Florida's long-term vigor. The Fire & Water Nature Trail takes you through many of the ecosystems found in the state forest. Accompanying interpretive information explains the importance of fire and water to the landscape. Be aware that hunting is allowed in the forest, so check ahead of time for hunt dates.

Live oaks shade picnic tables at the trailhead and make for an attractive pre- or post-dining spot. The hike begins amid a sandhill forest. These forests, comprised primarily of longleaf pines with wiregrass understory, were heavily logged a century ago. Without proper fire management, along with changeover from natural forest to urbanized uses, the longleaf/wiregrass habitat has been greatly reduced, along with plant and animal species that call it home. Therefore, the Jennings State Forest serves as an important natural oasis in greater Jacksonville.

The path is marked with painted blazes and is easy to follow. Work the margin between the sandhill forest and thickly wooded wetlands, composed primarily of bay trees and known as a baygall. The primary trees in this habitat are the sweetbay magnolia (the largest), along with understory trees, the loblolly bay and red bay. Following the beginning loop portion of the hike, a spur trail leads right to a wildlife blind. If you decide to take the spur trail to the blind, be quiet; plant yourself between the wooden fences cut with narrow sight lines; and be patient! If you are still and quiet and give it some time, you may see some critters of the state forest. Likely candidates are deer, turkeys, and armadillos. Birders may get lucky. Did I say you need to be quiet and patient? I have seen deer here myself.

The loop continues northwesterly toward Wheeler Branch. Note the longleaf pines making a comeback with proper fire management. Pass a seepage slope and an opportunity to see

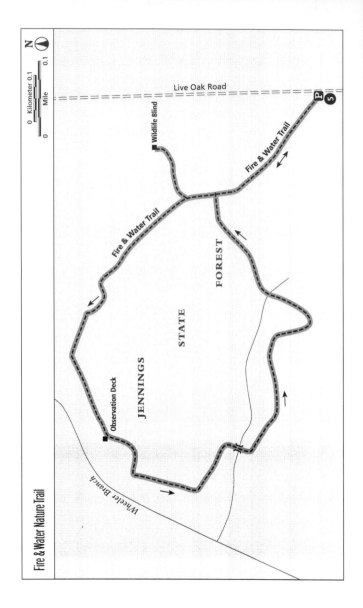

some pitcher plants, still traveling the border of sandhill and thicker, wetter woodland. The path curves southerly as it joins a hill dropping to Wheeler Branch. Grab a view from an observation deck into the steeply sloped stream valley, where serpentine Wheeler Branch flows under Southern magnolias. Repose benches beckon. Travel along the stream.

The trek climbs away from Wheeler Branch only to drop and span one of its tributaries. This feeder branch flows steeply off the sandhills and spills noisily under the bridge, adding audio appeal to your walk. The path makes an easterly track primarily in pines, but does cross the head of that tributary one more time. Wander through eye-appealing woods and then backtrack after completing the loop portion of your hike.

Miles and Directions

0.0   Leave the trailhead, walking around a pole gate, passing a kiosk. Join a wide track bordered by turkey oaks and pines with scattered palmetto.

0.2   The trail splits. Begin the loop portion of the hike. Stay right so you can follow the numbered interpretive stops. Bisect a thickly wooded wetland.

0.3   Take a spur trail leading right under mixed forest to the wildlife blind. Backtrack to the main loop.

0.6   Curve around a seepage slope with a colony of pitcher plants nearby.

0.9   Reach an observation deck extending toward Wheeler Branch. Look down on the precipitous wooded slope to the sand-bottomed blackwater streamlet.

1.1   Make a sharp right turn and descend to bridge a tributary of Wheeler Branch. Travel easterly along the line between the stream woods to your left and pines to your right.

1.4   Step over the head of a seepage slope, bordered by cane.

1.6   Complete the loop portion of the hike. Turn right here and backtrack toward the trailhead.

1.8   Arrive back at the trailhead.

6 Black Creek Ravines Hike

This trek travels through a protected swath of lower Black Creek. Here, make a double loop in hilly terrain, passing sensitive seepage slopes and making Black Creek, where you can enjoy views of the waterway from an oak bluff. The final part of the hike passes two ravine observation points, allowing a good look into this increasingly rare natural community.

Distance: 4.4-mile double loop
Approximate hiking time: 2 to 3 hours
Difficulty: Moderate due to hills and distance
Trail surface: Natural surfaces
Best season: Oct through Apr
Other trail users: Equestrians
Canine compatibility: Leashed dogs permitted

Fees and permits: No fees or permits required
Schedule: Sunrise to sunset
Maps: Black Creek Ravines Conservation Area, USGS Middleburg
Trail contacts: St. Johns River Water Management District, 7775 Baymeadows Way, Ste. 102, Jacksonville, FL 32256; (904) 730-6270; www.sjrwmd.com

Finding the trailhead: From exit 12 on I-295 southwest of downtown, take Blanding Boulevard (SR 21) south for 13 miles to Clay County Road 218 on the south side of Middleburg. Turn left on CR 218 east and follow it for 2 miles, then turn left on Green Road. Follow Green Road for 0.8 mile to the trailhead on your right. (**Note:** You will see an initial trailhead at 0.6 mile under some power lines; this is alternate parking.) The better parking and primary trailhead is 0.2 mile farther. Official trailhead address: 5663 Green Rd., Middleburg, FL 32258. GPS trailhead coordinates: 30.058056, -81.846750

The Hike

We are fortunate that St. Johns River Water Management decided to purchase and preserve this scenic tract just outside of Middleburg. Here, Black Creek is making a major bend around steep sandhills. Drainages cut ravines in the sandhills leading to Black Creek. Elevations range from 90 feet at its highest point to 5 feet above sea level at Black Creek, by Florida standards a major elevation differential. The draining of the high sandhills has created deep wooded ravines and seepage slopes, which are uncommon communities and thus are protected by the conservation area.

Furthermore, the 973-acre tract also functions as a water recharge area for Black Creek and the greater St. Johns River. Over 2.7 miles of water frontage on Black Creek are kept in a natural state. Part of this hike travels along the south shore of Black Creek, and a spur trail leads from the loop to a backcountry campsite located on conservation area property.

There are a total of three loops at Black Creek Ravines and they are blazed in white, yellow, and red. As a whole the trail system is well marked and maintained. It uses a combination of single-track and double-track paths. In some places, since equestrians also ply the trails, the trail track will be looser.

The hike itself explores the conservation area through two connected loops. Travel through mixed pine and oak woods, heading northbound. Make a trail junction and an alternate loop hike extends to the east side of the property. Our loop, however, continues north, skirting a seepage slope. It then begins its second loop, passing under a power line before reaching Black Creek. Here you can gain a bluff-top view of the alluring dark stream, which is quite wide at this point.

Travel along the shoreline, gaining more views before climbing the path away from the water. The second half of

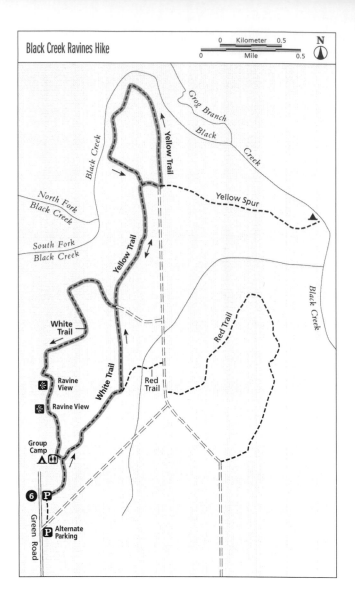

Black Creek Ravines Hike

the hike provides the best vantages of the ravines for which the conservation area is named. Here the path travels along the edge of the sandhills and the drop-off into the ravines. Two designated observation points allow you to safely peer down into the surprisingly steep plant communities, which contrast greatly with the sandhills up top. The narrow ravines allow more shade, and the increased moisture creates luxuriant plant communities. But it's not all about plants; you may also see deer, gopher, tortoises, and bird life here at the ravines.

Miles and Directions

0.0 From the parking area, join the single-track White Trail as it enters rich oak woodland.

0.2 Make a trail junction. This is the beginning of the actual White Trail loop. Stay right, heading northeast. A group campsite and restroom are visible off to your left. The level track belies nearby ravines.

0.6 Reach a trail junction in oaks. Here, the Red Trail makes a separate 2.5-mile loop. Stay left with the White Trail, heading north.

0.9 Intersect the Yellow Trail. The White Trail heads left and will be your return route. Keep straight on a downgrade and skirt the edge of a seep. Briefly open onto a power line before returning to woods.

1.5 Reach the loop portion of the Yellow Trail. Turn right here, heading to the east side of the power lines and meet the Yellow Spur. Turn left and follow the road heading north under the easternmost power lines, passing astride a hardwood swamp on either side of the power lines. The Yellow Spur goes easterly 0.7 mile to a backcountry campsite along Black Creek.

2.1 Come alongside the shoreline of Black Creek. Make a bluff-top cruise above the cypress-lined shoreline.

2.3 Leave the waterway, passing through moist oak woods before climbing.

2.5 Complete the Yellow Trail loop. Begin backtracking, still on the Yellow Trail.

3.1 Meet the White Trail. This time turn right, walking the margin between sandhill and seepage slope.

3.8 Come to the first ravine observation point.

3.9 Reach the second ravine observation point.

4.1 Complete the White Trail loop near the group campsite and restroom. Stay left and backtrack toward the trailhead.

4.4 Arrive back at the trailhead.

7 Ortega Stream Valley Trail

This trail leads through verdant oak woodland and is located at Ringhaver Park, operated by the city of Jacksonville. The thick, shady forest allows year-round hiking. Reach a spur trail where an elevated boardwalk avails a top-down view of a freshwater hardwood swamp before reaching a dock on the Ortega River. Enjoy the aquatic aspect of the trek before returning to the trailhead.

Distance: 1.6-mile balloon loop
Approximate hiking time: 1 to 1.5 hours
Difficulty: Easy
Trail surface: Asphalt
Best season: Year-round
Other trail users: Paddlers
Canine compatibility: Leashed dogs permitted

Fees and permits: No fees or permits required
Schedule: 7:30 a.m. to dusk
Maps: Ortega Stream Valley Trail @Ringhaver Trail Map; USGS Orange Park
Trail contacts: Ringhaver Park, 5198 118th St., Jacksonville, FL 32244; (904) 255-7919; www .jaxparks.com

Finding the trailhead: From exit 16 on I-295 southwest of downtown, take SR 134 east for 1 mile to a red light and Blanding Boulevard (SR 21). Turn right on SR 21 and follow it for 1 mile to 118th Street. Turn left on 118th Street and follow it east for 1.4 miles to Ringhaver Park, on your right. Turn into the park on Ortega Farms Boulevard, and follow it 0.3 mile to the trailhead parking just before the tennis courts. GPS trailhead coordinates: 30.229258, 81.715844

The Hike

Ringhaver Park, run by the city of Jacksonville, is a large multipurpose facility, seemingly with a little something for everyone—including hikers. It offers tennis and pickleball courts, playgrounds, ball fields, and picnic facilities, all situated on the west bank of the Ortega River, which has its origin as a stream starting in far western Duval County. Though much of the park is developed, a large swath of hardwood swamp and woodland close to the Ortega River remains in a natural state.

The Ortega Stream Valley Trail travels through a portion of this natural area, offering undeveloped beauty to complement the developed park facilities. However, after coming here you will wish the trail system was expanded to include more of the natural area. If you desire a longer hike, simply walk the trail a couple of times or more, as is done by the many regulars who use this path for their daily exercise. In addition to hikers, paddlers also use the trail to access the canoe/kayak launch located on the Ortega River, so don't be surprised if you see someone carrying a boat on the hiking trail!

A small shady gazebo marks the trail's beginning. Thick woods with an overstory of pine are complemented by bountiful oaks and maple. Dense undergrowth and dangling vines indicate that it's been a long time since these fire-dependent woods have burned. Since Ringhaver is an urban park bordered on three sides by residences, it is unlikely that fire will be used to maintain the natural character of the woods; thus, it is likely they will remain thick and completely convert to an oak-dominated hardwood forest.

A wetter part of the woodland through which the trail passes is dominated by bay trees—sweetbay magnolia and red bay. A few areas are open and sandy, while other spots have regal live oaks towering overhead. You'll also notice a few sand trails that spur on and off the asphalt loop. If you stay with the asphalt, you can't get lost. Make sure and take the 1,000-foot boardwalk to the Ortega River—it's the highlight of the hike.

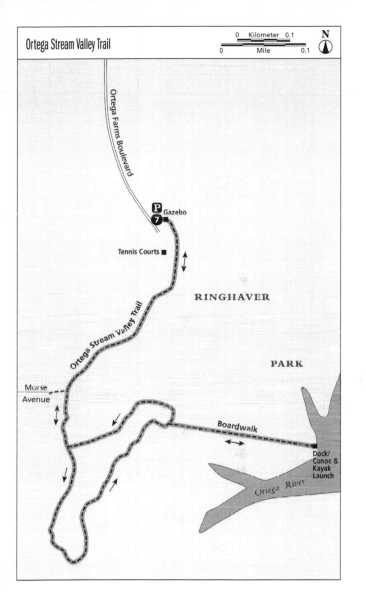

Ortega Stream Valley Trail

Ortega Farms Boulevard

P
7 Gazebo

Tennis Courts ■

RINGHAVER

Ortega Stream Valley Trail

PARK

Morse
Avenue

Boardwalk

Dock/
Canoe &
Kayak
Launch

Ortega River

0   Kilometer 0.1
0   Mile   0.1

N

Maples, sweetgums, and other hardwoods form the nucleus of the swamp. Late fall is a good time to walk the boardwalk and see these trees in their autumn finery. Spring is also a good time to visit and see the colorful buds before they transform into green leaves. Consider bringing binoculars as the boardwalk is also a good birding location; since it's situated near the water, you can view shorebirds, but it's also in the swamp, where the elevated perch will increase your chances of seeing songbirds.

Since this part of the Ortega River is tidally influenced, the floating dock is designed to rise and lower with the tides, yet it allows easy access to the water no matter the tidal time. This is where paddlers launch, floating out from the inlet in front of you to explore the main river. Consider bringing a watercraft of your own and doubling your fun here at Ringhaver Park.

Miles and Directions

0.0   Pick up the asphalt path leaving south from a small gazebo next to the parking area. Shortly curve behind the tennis courts, entering thick woods.

0.2   Reach a boardwalk over wetland forest. Just ahead a spur trail leads right, connecting to a neighborhood on Morse Avenue. The Ortega Stream Valley Trail continues on another boardwalk.

0.3   Reach the loop portion of the hike. Keep forward here as your return route comes in on the left. Pass through a live-oak copse.

0.5   The loop curves back to the north after reaching the south end of the park.

0.8   Reach a trail junction. Turn right. Here, an asphalt path soon reaches the elevated boardwalk. Climb the wooden walkway and enjoy your perch as you travel easterly through a hardwood swamp. The boardwalk ends at a dock. Enjoy watery views of the Ortega River. Backtrack.

1.2   Continue the primary loop, traveling through more oaks.

1.3   Complete the loop. Backtrack toward the trailhead.

1.6   Arrive back at the trailhead and finish the hike.

8 Blue Cypress Park Hike

This Jacksonville city park hike takes you along the shores of the St. Johns River and out to a pier with a great view of downtown Jacksonville and beyond. It also loops into a towering maritime hammock rife with live oaks. The first part of the hike travels among developed facilities at this multipurpose preserve.

Distance: 2.4-mile double loop
Approximate hiking time: 1 to 2 hours
Difficulty: Easy
Trail surface: Asphalt and natural surfaces
Best season: Oct through Apr
Other trail users: None
Canine compatibility: Leashed dogs permitted

Fees and permits: No fees or permits required
Schedule: Sunrise to sunset
Maps: None; USGS Arlington, Eastport
Trail contacts: Blue Cypress Park, 4012 University Blvd. North, Jacksonville, FL 32202; (904) 255-7919; www.jaxparks .oom

Finding the trailhead: From the Merrill Road / Jacksonville University exit on SR 9A northeast of downtown, take Merrill Road west for 2.8 miles to University Boulevard. Turn right on University Boulevard and follow it for 1.7 miles to Blue Cypress Park, on your left. Enter the loop road and park near the community center. GPS trailhead coordinates: 30.374647, -81.608395

The Hike

Once known primarily for its golf course, Blue Cypress Park has since been transformed into more of a multipurpose facility, with an added emphasis on its natural features. In fact, the former eighteen-hole course was reduced to nine holes, then closed, then reopened in 2021. Originally part of the

Edenfield Estates housing development, the environmentally sensitive and scenic 118-acre tract was purchased by the city. It is set on the eastern bank of the St. Johns River, north of downtown, on land that would go for astronomical prices these days, for its river views alone.

Most of the urban shoreline of greater Jacksonville has been developed, yet this park offers an unspoiled stretch where you not only can travel out to a pier over the river, but also hike a boardwalk that runs along the St. Johns. In addition, you can access the grass shoreline, punctuated with small beach areas, from breaks in the boardwalk. A gorgeous live-oak hardwood hammock rises away from the river, and this hike makes a loop through the heart of it. The asphalt trail is 6 to 8 feet wide in the developed part of the park. The undeveloped part of the park utilizes natural surfaces, but be careful: The trail segment in the live-oak hammock is somewhat rooty, so watch your footing.

The beginning of the hike makes a loop near the developed facilities—a park inspection tour, if you will. Along the way you'll pass the old golf clubhouse—now a community center; you'll also pass a lake, playground, soccer fields, and tennis courts. The trail then heads west away from the developed facilities and cruises through some of the remaining golf course before reaching the fishing pier and boardwalk. Span a tidal creek bordered by marsh grasses. This is a good birding area. The flow of the water in the tidal creek will reveal whether the tide is coming in or going out. Scattered pines and cedars gain purchase in the sandy soil.

Upon leaving the St. Johns, the path enters a maritime hammock complete with palms, Southern magnolia, sweetbay magnolia, and live oaks draped in Spanish moss, forming a green cathedral. The now-natural-surface path snakes throughout

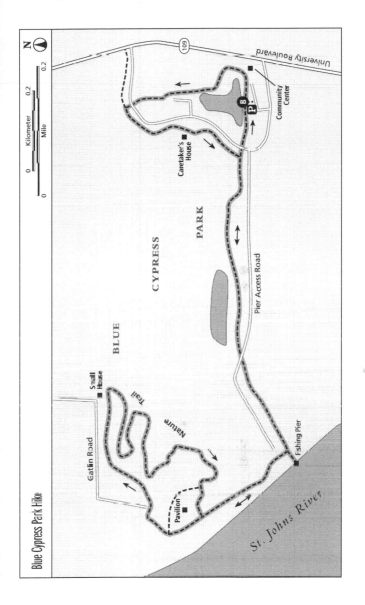

Blue Cypress Park Hike

the hammock, making the most of the available terrain, then emerges along the open St. Johns River shoreline where you can gain one last view before backtracking to the trailhead.

Miles and Directions

0.0 From the community center parking area, take the asphalt path heading easterly toward University Boulevard. Begin circling the park lake, passing the old clubhouse, now a community center. Ahead, the path takes you by a play area and tennis courts.

0.1 Cross the park road and reach a trail junction. Here a short asphalt path leads right to University Boulevard. This hike leads left and goes near the park caretaker's house.

0.5 Reach an intersection near Pier Access Road. Turn right on the asphalt path, now heading westerly into a thick forest with especially tall trees. The woods give way to a grassy field astride the golf course.

0.7 Cross the fishing pier access road after passing a small pond. Continue west, aiming for the St. Johns River.

0.8 Reach the fishing pier and boardwalk. Head out to the pier, enjoying first-rate views of the St. Johns River, port facilities, and downtown Jacksonville. A small gazebo shades the pier's end. Now, walk north on the boardwalk running parallel with the St. Johns River.

1.1 A spur trail leads right to a covered pavilion. This will be your return route. The boardwalk soon gives way, allowing easy access to the shoreline. At lower tides small sand beaches will be exposed. Shortly pass a second spur trail leading right toward the pavilion.

1.2 Reach an alternate parking area accessed from Gatlin Road. You are now in a maritime hardwood hammock. The trail begins winding through the lush woods, circling near a small house.

1.9 Emerge at the pavilion near the St. Johns River. Travel toward the St. Johns and then pick up the boardwalk and begin backtracking.

2.4 Return to the community center trailhead and complete the hike.

⑨ Hammock Trail at Fort Caroline

This hike at Fort Caroline National Monument explores a hilly maritime forest before dropping to the St. Johns River and the site of a French bastion from the 1500s. Enjoy not only the human history but also the natural beauty of this shoreline. Give yourself ample time to not only hike the trail, but also to explore the fort and stop in at the visitor center.

Distance: 1.2-mile loop
Approximate hiking time: 1 to 1.5 hours
Difficulty: Easy, but has hills
Trail surface: Natural surfaces
Best season: Oct through Apr
Other trail users: None
Canine compatibility: Leashed dogs permitted
Fees and permits: No fees or permits required

Schedule: 9 a.m. to 4:30 p.m.
Maps: Fort Caroline & Theodore Roosevelt Area, USGS Mayport, Eastport
Trail contacts: Timucuan Ecological and Historic Preserve, 12713 Fort Caroline Rd., Jacksonville, FL 32225; (904) 641-7155; www.nps.gov/timu

Finding the trailhead: From the Monument Road exit on SR 9A east of downtown, take Monument Road east for 4 miles to meet Fort Caroline Road. Turn right on Fort Caroline Road and follow it for 0.1 mile, then turn left, staying with Fort Caroline Road, as Mount Pleasant Road heads straight. Next, turn left toward the Fort Caroline visitor center and reach the trailhead/visitor center parking area. GPS trailhead coordinates: 30.385669, -81.497811

The Hike

Fort Caroline National Memorial is part of the greater Timucuan Ecological and Historic Preserve, a sizable agglomeration of tidal waters and lands northeast of downtown Jacksonville. Run by the National Park Service, Fort Caroline preserves the approximate spot where French explorers established a colony in 1564. The original intent of the colony was to find riches such as those the Spaniards were bringing home from elsewhere in the New World, but it ended up having a religious factor as well, since the French Protestants, known as Huguenots, were being persecuted in France.

The colonists tried to carve out a living along the shores of the St. Johns but found the going tough in America. Though occupied by the Timucuan Indians, who were alternately friend and foe to the Huguenots, the lands were nevertheless claimed by the Spaniards, who attacked Fort Caroline in 1565, slaughtering most of the inhabitants before occupying the fort themselves. The French recaptured Fort Caroline but didn't attempt to colonize the area any further. Unfortunately, there are no remains of the actual fort itself, which may have been obliterated during the dredging of the St. Johns River. However, the approximate location is believed to be correct.

Today you can learn about the life ways of the colonists and the Timucuan Indians and about the greater ecological preserve at this visitor center, as well as hike the Hammock Trail, which wanders through a gorgeous maritime hammock forest. Travel over ancient shell mounds and dunes that give the hike some serious vertical variation. The Hammock Trail is a natural-surface path about 4 feet wide. The park service keeps this trail and the grounds of Fort Caroline shipshape, making for an eye-pleasing experience with no bad surprises. Contemplation benches await those willing to relax and absorb the atmosphere. Over two dozen interpretive information stops are stretched out along the loop, turning this hike into a human and natural history learning experience. The hike is described below in a clockwise direction, allowing you to save Fort Caroline and the St. Johns River for last.

Enter live-oak-dominated woodland where Spanish moss hangs on anything that doesn't move. Other oaks, huge pines,

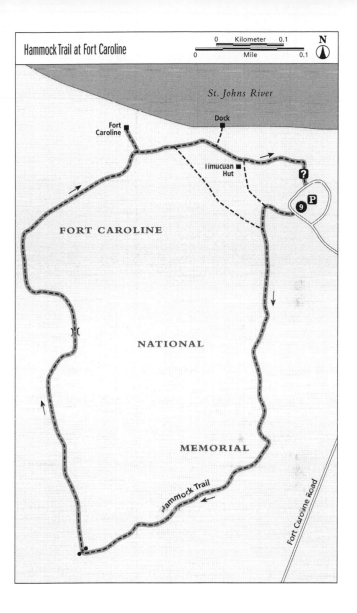

Hammock Trail at Fort Caroline

0   Kilometer   0.1

0   Mile   0.1

N

St. Johns River

Dock

Fort
Caroline

Timucuan
Hut

?

P

9

FORT CAROLINE

NATIONAL

MEMORIAL

Hammock Trail

Fort Caroline Road

hickory, Southern magnolia, sweetgum, wax myrtle, cedar, and still more trees comprise the high-canopied forest undulating over ancient sand dunes. After rolling through the hilly woods, the path wanders into marsh, bridging a tidal stream, which adds to the biodiversity of the hike. The hike leads to the Fort Caroline replica located along the St. Johns River, where you can walk among the earthworks, guns, and walls of the moat-encircled fort, imagining what it would be like to live here along the wide waterway. Take note of the huge pines near the fort. Several short nature paths give you various options to choose from on your return trip from the fort to the visitor center. Watch for the replica Timucuan hut on your way back.

Miles and Directions

0.0 As you face the visitor center, look left for the signed Hammock Trail trailhead. Shortly join a 4-foot-wide natural-surface path heading toward Fort Caroline, walking but a few feet to reach another trail junction. Here, a narrow connector trail leads left and downhill to join the actual Hammock Trail. Stay left with the Hammock Trail, heading south.

0.3 The loop makes a turn to the right, now heading southwest.

0.4 Top out on a hill after a solid climb. Begin descending to a gate, then turn right again, walking north for Fort Caroline and the St. Johns River.

0.7 Bridge a marshy tidal stream.

1.0 Emerge at the Fort Caroline replica after a short spur trail leading left. The original fort has been lost to time, but what you see now is a physical rendering using the maps and notes of Jacques Le Moyne, an artist and mapmaker who lived at the colony. Keep east on a wide trail, staying left, closest to the river, as a trail leads right back to the parking area.

1.1 Reach a spur trail leading left to a dock on the St. Johns.

1.2 Reach the visitor center, completing the hike.

10 Spanish Pond Loop

One of Jacksonville's finest day hikes, this trek travels over wooded ancient dunes of a maritime hammock onto even hillier Timucuan shell mounds, past a hermit's cabin, to an observation point overlooking a salt marsh along the St. Johns. Your return trip passes a Confederate soldier's grave and then reaches a high point and vista before returning to the trailhead.

Distance: 2.9-mile balloon loop
Approximate hiking time: 2 to 2.5 hours
Difficulty: Moderate due to hills
Trail surface: Natural surfaces
Best season: Oct through Apr
Other trail users: None
Canine compatibility: Leashed dogs permitted

Fees and permits: No fees or permits required
Schedule: 9 a.m. to 4:30 p.m.
Maps: Fort Caroline & Theodore Roosevelt Area, USGS Mayport
Trail contacts: Timucuan Ecological and Historic Preserve, 12713 Fort Caroline Rd., Jacksonville, FL 32225; (904) 641-7155; www.nps.gov/timu

Finding the trailhead: From the Monument Road exit on SR 9A east of downtown, take Monument Road east for 4 miles to meet Fort Caroline Road. Turn right on Fort Caroline Road and follow it for 0.1 mile, then turn left, staying with Fort Caroline Road, as Mount Pleasant Road heads straight. Next, turn left toward the Fort Caroline visitor center and instead of turning left into the visitor center, turn right to the Fort Caroline picnic area. GPS trailhead coordinates: 30.384167, -81.495750

The Hike

The Theodore Roosevelt Area of the Timucuan Ecological and Historic Preserve covers 600 acres of maritime hammock, salt marshes, and incredible shell mounds, deposited by the Timucuan Indians. A quality trail system has been integrated into the tract. The beauty of the area was recognized by a man named Willie Browne, who resided here nearly all his born days before turning his land over to the Nature Conservancy so it could be left in its natural state and enjoyed by others.

This hike travels by Browne's cabin site, a small clearing in the forest. Just a few moments at his retreat will persuade you to see his point of view. Browne's arrival at this spot was accidental, a simple twist of fate. Early in the 1900s Browne's parents moved to Jacksonville from New York City. They had settled down in Florida when a yellow fever epidemic swept across Jacksonville; they came out to this land near Fort Caroline to escape the disease. Willie and his brother Saxon grew to love life in their neck of the woods, and fashioned a living through fishing, timbering, and more. Browne saw the vast urbanization around him and couldn't bear the thought of this spot being turned into condos. Fortunately, it didn't happen, and Browne lived more than eighty years before passing away.

The hike begins on the Spanish Pond Trail, aiming for the observation tower on the marshes of the St. Johns. The heavily wooded path first meanders along its namesake body of water, a good birding area mostly screened by vegetation. As is the case here in Florida, the slightest elevation changes alter the forest composition: Pines and palmettos occupy their place on higher ground, but the junglesque maritime hammock of live oak, Southern magnolia, palms, and cedars are most common. Ancient sand dunes and shell mounds lend vertical variation. Sand live oaks find their place on the hills.

Take time to repose at Willie Browne's cabin site before heading out to a strand of land and the wooden observation tower. Higher tides may inundate part of the path. At the tower, you can look out on the salt marsh of the St. Johns River and back toward the wooded shell mounds the Timucuans called home for thousands of years.

Your return route travels past the grave of Confederate soldier Sergeant John Nathan Spearing on the Timucuan Trail. It then takes you up a ridge of shells atop the marsh where you will enjoy great views of the marsh and beyond.

Miles and Directions

0.0   Leave the shaded parking area on the Spanish Pond Trail and immediately join a boardwalk that leads to a natural-surface trail. Head right, as the trail going left accesses another part of the parking area.

0.1   Reach another of many boardwalks over part-time wetlands. Where the boardwalk isn't present, the maritime hammock in these bottoms will have a rooty track. Watch your feet while also enjoying the immense beauty of the area.

0.8   Meet the Timucuan Trail coming in from your left. This will be your return route. For now, stay right, descending from a hill, still on the Spanish Pond Trail. The track shortly widens.

1.0   Come to a four-way junction. Here, the Willie Browne Trail comes in from the right. The trail going left shortcuts over to the Timucuan Trail. Keep straight, still on the Spanish Pond Trail.

1.1   Climb a hill and reach the Willie Browne cabin site and another trail junction. Here, another arm of the Willie Browne Trail leaves right to an alternate parking area off Mount Pleasant Road. A single-track path leaves left to the Timucuan Trail. Keep forward toward the observation tower.

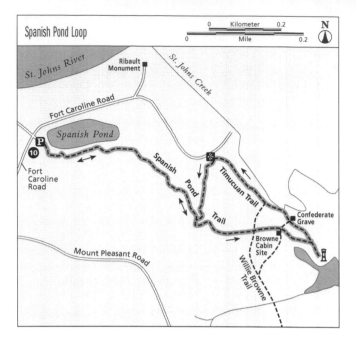

1.3 Reach and climb the observation tower after passing the Timucuan Trail and traveling a slender cedar-covered spit. Backtrack, then join the Timucuan Trail.

1.4 Pass the grave of Confederate soldier, Sergeant John Nathan Spearing. A spur trail leads left, back to the Browne cabin site.

1.5 An alternate path leads to the Willie Browne Trail. Keep climbing.

1.8 Come to a high point and view of the Timucuan lands below. Your best views are to the north. Drop off the hill on a sandy track in scrubby oaks.

2.1 Meet the Spanish Pond Trail. Turn right and backtrack.

2.9 Arrive back at the trailhead, completing the hike.

11 Cedar Point Preserve

Make a fine loop at this component of the greater 7 Creeks Recreation Area. Leave Cedar Point Road, then head south, passing the old Anderson Cemetery. Enjoy a live oak hammock, then make your way to a view of the Fitzpatrick Creek marshes before looping near Pumpkin Hill Creek. After hiking at Cedar Point Preserve once you are sure to return and trek the balance of the trails in this 618-acre preserve.

Distance: 3.6-mile loop with spurs
Approximate hiking time: 1.5 to 2 hours
Difficulty: Moderate
Trail surface: Natural surfaces
Best season: Oct through Apr
Other trail users: Bicyclers, equestrians
Canine compatibility: Leashed dogs permitted

Fees and permits: None
Schedule: Sunrise to sunset
Maps: Cedar Point Preserve, USGS Mayport
Trail contacts: Cedar Point Preserve, 7116 Cedar Point Rd., Jacksonville, FL 32226; (904) 630-2489; www.timucuanparks .org

Finding the trailhead: From exit 40 on I-295 northeast of downtown, take Alta Drive north for 1.2 miles, then keep straight as it becomes Yellow Bluff Road. Follow it another 0.7 mile, then turn right onto New Berlin Road. Follow New Berlin Road east a mile, then stay straight as it becomes Cedar Point Road. Continue east 4.6 miles and the trailhead will be on your right. Official trailhead address: 7222 Cedar Point Road, Jacksonville, FL 32226. GPS trailhead coordinates: 30.462143, -81.488534

The Hike

Cedar Point Preserve is an important tract linking local, state, and federal parks in the tidal streams, marshes, and maritime forests of the greater 5,600-acre 7 Creeks Recreation Area, northeast of Jacksonville. The recreation area provides a haven for the flora and fauna of northeast Florida as well as over 30 miles of hiking trails for outdoor enthusiasts like us. The 7 Creeks Recreation Area is bordered by the even larger Timucuan Ecological and Historic Preserve. Trails link these various lands, including the pathway upon which this hike begins—the 7 Creeks Trail.

The 7 Creeks Trail (7 miles in length, too) starts up at Betz-Tiger Preserve (another fine hiking destination) then heads south through Pumpkin Hill Creek Preserve State Park into Cedar Point Preserve, where we pick up the track, then across a fine bridge to Cedar Point, run by the National Park Service.

Our hike will take it past the Anderson Cemetery, where Civil War veterans are interred, just one visual reminder of this historic ground, then make a circuit through Cedar Point Preserve, traversing deep woods on the Turkey Trot Trail before heading to an overlook of the marshes of Fitzpatrick Creek. From there, work easterly through eye-pleasing forest to make your way to the margin where the forest borders the marshes of Pumpkin Hill Creek. A final backtrack completes the adventure. Next time you can try other trails at Cedar Point Preserve.

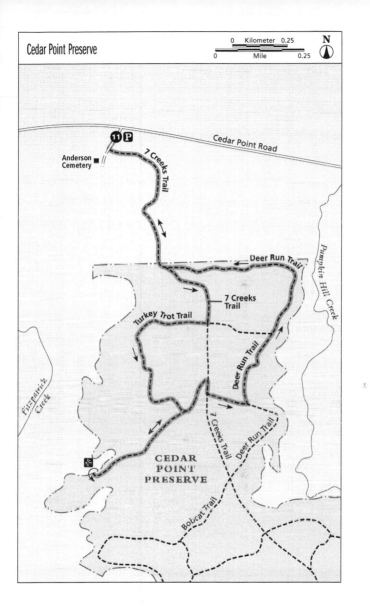

Cedar Point Preserve

0 Kilometer 0.25
0 Mile 0.25

N

Cedar Point Road

11 P

Anderson Cemetery

7 Creeks Trail

Deer Run Trail

Pumpkin Hill Creek

7 Creeks Trail

Turkey Trot Trail

Deer Run Trail

Fitzpatrick Creek

7 Creeks Trail

Deer Run Trail

CEDAR POINT PRESERVE

Bobcat Trail

Miles and Directions

0.0 Leave the Fitzpatrick trailhead south, in a disjunct tract of Pumpkin Hill Creek Preserve State Park, hiking along a fence line on the 7 Creeks Trail. Reach a kiosk. The Anderson Cemetery is to your right. Stay with the 7 Creeks Trail in mixed woods of wax myrtle, oak, and pine, above thickets of palmetto.

0.3 Stay left as a service road leaves right.

0.5 Reach a gate and officially enter Cedar Creek Preserve. Stay with the 7 Creeks Trail as a service road splits away. Just ahead the Deer Run Trail, your return route, leaves left. Continue in deep woods of live oak, laurel oak, pine, and palmetto.

0.8 At a four-way intersection, split right with the Turkey Trot Trail. Hike west on a narrower track. Shortly pass a seasonal pond on your left.

1.3 Take the spur trail right toward Fitzpatrick Creek. Skirt along the nexus of woodland and marsh.

1.6 Reach the all-natural view into the marshes of Fitzpatrick Creek. Backtrack.

1.9 Return to the Turkey Trot Trail, keeping northeasterly.

2.1 Intersect the 7 Creeks Trail. Head right (south), then take a quick left onto a white-blazed connector trail.

2.3 Meet the Deer Run Trail. Head left (northwest) in lush forest rich with magnolia and live oak. The brightness through the trees to the east is the open marsh of Pumpkin Hill Creek.

2.5 Pass a connector trail heading left (west). Stay straight (north) with the Deer Run Trail.

2.7 The Deer Run Trail curves left (west) near the preserve boundary. Cruise through tall pines.

3.1 Return to the 7 Creeks Trail, completing the loop part of the hike. Head right (north) backtracking toward the trailhead.

3.6 Arrive back at the trailhead, completing the adventure.

12 Pumpkin Hill Creek Preserve Hike

This lesser heralded Florida state park offers a loop hike through a variety of plant communities. The trek traces double-track paths through rare oak scrub, pine flatwoods, maritime hammock, and to vistas of tidal, marsh-bordered Pumpkin Hill Creek.

Distance: 2.1-mile loop with spurs
Approximate hiking time: 1 to 2 hours
Difficulty: Easy
Trail surface: Natural surfaces
Best season: Oct through Apr
Other trail users: Bicyclists and equestrians
Canine compatibility: Leashed dogs permitted

Fees and permits: No fees or permits required
Schedule: 8 a.m. to sunset
Maps: Pumpkin Hill Creek Preserve State Park, USGS Mayport
Trail contacts: Pumpkin Hill Creek Preserve State Park, 13802 Pumpkin Hill Rd., Jacksonville, FL 32226; (904) 696-5980; www .FloridaStateParks.org

Finding the trailhead: From SR 9A east of downtown, take Heckscher Drive a short distance east to New Berlin Road. Turn left on New Berlin Road and follow it for 3.7 miles to Cedar Point Road. Turn right on Cedar Point Road and follow it for 4.6 miles to Pumpkin Hill Road. Turn left on Pumpkin Hill Road and follow it for 0.8 mile to turn left into the trailhead parking area. GPS trailhead coordinates: 30.473667, -81.487222

The Hike

Pumpkin Hill Creek, in the far northeastern reaches of Duval County, used to be the back of beyond, but the tentacles of Jacksonville continue stretching that way. Ironically, with more people you need more green spaces; thus, the St. Johns River Water Management District, the city of Jacksonville, and the state of Florida pooled their money to purchase nearly 4,000 acres along the west shore of Pumpkin Hill Creek, a tidal marsh stream. The land has undergone many uses. Long ago, vast stands of old-growth slash pine were turpentined. The sap from the evergreens was collected when men made an incision in the bark and installed a V-shaped metal plate, which helped pine sap drain into a pottery-type cup. The sap was then distilled into rosin and turpentine. A new slit was made each year in the trees, just a little lower than the year before, creating what was known as a "cat face." Later, the same trees were cut down for wood when the area was timbered. Still later, the land became a private hunting preserve, and oysters were processed at a location on Pumpkin Hill Creek.

Today, Pumpkin Hill Creek Preserve is a large wildland where you can hear the wind blow through the pines, see songbirds jumping from branch to branch in oak scrub, watch deer browse beneath a live oak, or paddle your canoe/kayak along the open marshes. Land managers are working hard to restore the native plants and animals to the area. Fire is an important component of the habitat restoration. The numerous sand roads on the tract are effective divisions used to manage the preserve.

Additional trails have been added since the park's inception. Also, the park trail system has been linked to Tiger-Betz

Preserve to the north and Cedar Point Preserve to the south, using the long-distance 7 Creeks Trail. In fact, Pumpkin Hill Preserve State Park is a component of the greater 7 Creeks Recreation Area. Our route follows already-established fire roads, but dedicated hiking trails are also available.

This hike travels to two vistas overlooking Pumpkin Hill Creek as it makes a loop through the property. The adventure immediately enters its signature environment—flatwoods scrub. The scrub oak trees that grow here are important bird habitats. Oak scrub is one of the most endangered habitats in Florida because it is so easily developed and little of it remains. Widely scattered pines rise above the low canopy. Ahead, the oak scrub gives way to palmetto prairie pocked with pines.

The hike turns north and then east. A spur trail leads to Pumpkin Hill Creek, where you can relax under live oaks while looking over the tidal stream bordered in marsh grasses. The loop carries you back to the trailhead, but you're not done yet. Head east across Pumpkin Hill Creek Road to reach a second overlook of Pumpkin Hill Creek. The tidal stream flows through a wide expanse of marsh grasses bordered by woodland on the far side. Anglers or paddlers may be seen here. Backtrack to the trailhead. On your next visit try some of the dedicated hiking trails and create some circuits of your own.

Miles and Directions

0.0 Leave the large parking area and pass around a pole gate to head westerly into low oak scrub. The park office is visible to your left. Travel a sandy double-track.

0.3 Reach a trail junction. Here, turn acutely right on the 7 Creeks Trail while the other trails keep forward, then split just

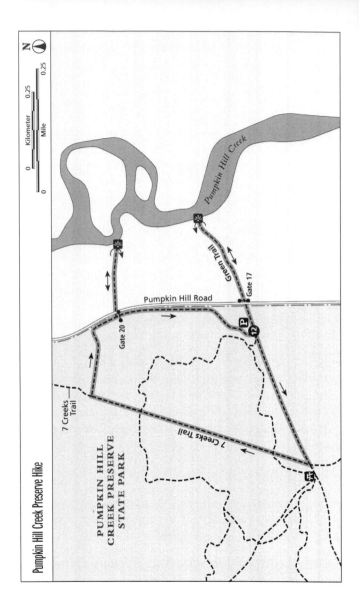

Pumpkin Hill Creek Preserve Hike

ahead near a picnic area. Begin traveling northeast in pine flatwoods. A dedicated hiking trail crosses the 7 Creeks Trail.

0.5 A closed road comes in from the left.

0.8 Turn right at a signed junction while sand roads keep forward. Now travel easterly toward Pumpkin Hill Road.

0.9 Meet Pumpkin Hill Road. Turn right on a fire line, then reach a Gate 20 and cross Pumpkin Hill Road. Take the spur path heading easterly, passing through Gate 19.

1.1 Reach Pumpkin Hill Creek in a live-oak copse. This is a scenic shaded area ideal for stopping. Backtrack and cross Pumpkin Hill Road, resuming a southerly track along a fence line before curving away from it.

1.5 Reach the parking area. Take the park entrance road east; cross Pumpkin Hill Road, then join the Green Trail after passing through Gate 17.

1.8 Come to the second overlook of Pumpkin Hill Creek. Backtrack to the trailhead.

2.1 Return to the trailhead and complete the hike.

13 Fort Clinch Bicycle Trail

Don't be discouraged by the word *bicycle* in this trail's name. The scenic path is open to hikers and is one of the better treks in the Jacksonville sphere. The popular hike travels a slender but long loop through maritime hardwood hammock forest on (nearly) continuously undulating terrain.

Distance: 6-mile loop

Approximate hiking time: 3 to 3.5 hours

Difficulty: More challenging due to hills and distance

Trail surface: Natural surfaces, a little road walking

Best season: Oct through Apr

Other trail users: Bicyclists and runners

Canine compatibility: Leashed dogs permitted

Fees and permits: Entrance fee required

Schedule: 8 a.m. to sunset

Maps: Fort Clinch State Park, USGS Fernandina Beach

Trail contacts: Fort Clinch State Park, 2601 Atlantic Ave., Fernandina Beach, FL 32034; (904) 277-7274; www .FloridaStateParks.org

Finding the trailhead: From exit 373 on I-95 north of Jacksonville, take SR A1A 16 miles easterly to the town of Fernandina Beach. Once in town A1A becomes 8th Street. Stay on 8th Street to meet Atlantic Avenue. Turn right on Atlantic Avenue and follow it for 2 miles to reach the state park, on your left. Enter the state park and stay with the main road for 3.3 miles to the Fort Clinch parking area. Pick up the trail on the east side of the entrance road just before you reach the main parking area. GPS trailhead coordinates: 30.703680, -81.452612

The Hike

This is a great hike. Located within the confines of Fort Clinch State Park, this trail leaves historic Fort Clinch—which you should visit either before or after this hike—and then heads south along a wooded dune line running through the heart of Amelia Island. The ups and downs are almost constant as the path crests these tree-covered dunes and then dips into swales, only to repeat the performance again and again. You finally reach the southernmost point of the trail, cross Fort Clinch Road, and curve back north. At this point the trail travels along the marshes of tidal Egan's Creek. This section is decidedly less hilly but does have sections of forested dunes, including one particularly high dune that offers a far-reaching vista to the west beyond the marshes of Egan's Creek.

Before becoming intimidated, realize that the majority of trail undulations are less than 20 feet up or down. It is the continuous nature of them that will test your mettle. Occasionally, the trail is forced to the road due to extremely sloping or wet terrain. These road walks are very short, however, but do provide you a means of shortcutting the loop should you choose not to do the entire 6 miles. Simply look across the road and you should be able to pick up the northbound section of the trail fairly easily. Bicyclists do use the trail, but they are asked by the state park to pedal in a given direction. Therefore, it is in your best interest to hike this loop in the opposite direction; that way, you will see and hear any oncoming bicyclists. (The park periodically changes the mandated bicycling direction.)

Upon leaving Fort Clinch the path enters verdant woodland of live oak, cedar, dahoon holly, palm, palmetto, and yaupon. The ups and downs are immediate and unremitting. Not all these undulations are the result of old dunes becoming forested; when the Civilian Conservation Corps developed this park, they dug many channels in an effort to rid the area of standing water and thus mosquitoes. They didn't realize that such ditches would eventually fill with soil and plant duff, rendering them useless. Now the trail crosses these occasional dug channels.

The sandy track can be very rooty in places, so watch your footing. Generally speaking, the sand path isn't too loose; because it is mixed with plant duff and is mostly shaded, it doesn't dry out easily. The hiking eases on the northbound track. Egan's Creek is plainly visible through the trees. Expect more climbs and descents, but you will be accustomed to these by hike's end.

Miles and Directions

0.0   Leave the Fort Clinch parking area and walk just a few feet back down Fort Clinch Road. Look left for a single-track footpath leaving the northeast side of the road, traveling the loop in a clockwise direction.

0.2   Pass a pair of live oaks with huge bases and widespread arms.

0.4   Saddle alongside a high wooded dune that forces the trail very close to the road.

0.8   Come near a brick oil storage tank left over from the early days of Fort Clinch. The oil was used to illuminate the fort lighthouses. The Willow Nature Trail trailhead is just across the road.

1.0   Pass under a small transmission line. Continue southeasterly.

1.3   Cross the access road to the Atlantic Beach Campground. Come near dug canals.

1.9   Cross a tidal streamlet near the Fort Clinch Road bridge. Continue in forest.

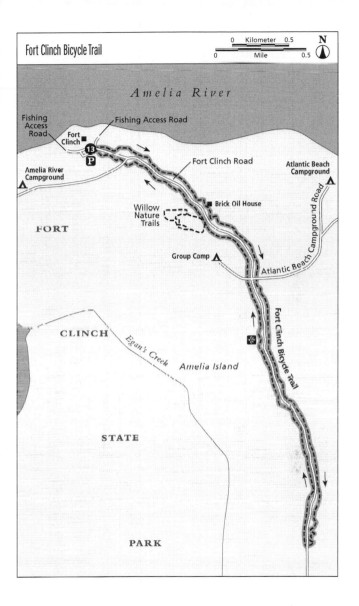

Fort Clinch Bicycle Trail

0   Kilometer   0.5
0   Mile   0.5

N

Amelia River

Fishing
Access
Road

Fishing Access Road

Fort
Clinch

13

P

Fort Clinch Road

Atlantic Beach
Campground

Amelia River
Campground

FORT

Willow
Nature
Trails

Brick Oil House

Atlantic Beach Campground Road

Group Camp

Atlantic Beach Campground Road

CLINCH

Egan's Creek

Amelia Island

Fort Clinch Bicycle Trail

STATE

PARK

2.3 Join Fort Clinch Road after slicing between wooded dunes.

2.4 Leave the road, reentering forest. Shortly rejoin the road.

2.5 Leave the road again, entering maritime woods.

3.0 Cross Fort Clinch Road. This is technically the trail's beginning but offers no parking. Turn northbound, with Egan's Creek to the west through the trees.

3.7 Climb a high dune with a good marsh vista.

3.9 Travel through an extended wetland.

4.1 Cross a tidal streamlet near the Fort Clinch Road bridge. Keep north.

4.7 Cross a sand service road leading to the park's group camp.

5.1 Bisect the Willow Nature Trail parking area. Stay with the trail closest to Fort Clinch Road.

5.8 Cross the road leading to Amelia River campground.

6.0 Emerge onto Fort Clinch parking area, completing the hike.

14 Dune Ridge Trail

Enjoy the best of Jacksonville's coastal islands on this hike at Little Talbot Island State Park. Start your trek near the Atlantic Ocean, then travel through rolling oceanside woodland before returning to the Atlantic. The rest of your hike is a sandy walk, where you travel along an unspoiled beach with good shelling opportunities.

Distance: 3.8-mile loop

Approximate hiking time: 2 to 2.5 hours

Difficulty: Moderate due to hills and potentially loose sand

Trail surface: Natural surfaces, a little asphalt

Best season: Oct through Apr

Other trail users: Bicyclists on trail part of hike

Canine compatibility: Leashed dogs permitted on forested portion of the hike, dogs prohibited on the beach

Fees and permits: Entrance fee required

Schedule: 8 a.m. to sunset

Maps: Dune Ridge Trail, USGS Mayport

Trail contacts: Little Talbot Island State Park, 12157 Heckscher Dr., Jacksonville, FL 32226; (904) 251-2320; www .FloridaStateParks.org

Finding the trailhead: From exit 358 on I-95 north of downtown, take FL 105 (Heckscher Drive) east for 22 miles to the state park entrance station. Be aware that after 20 miles, FL 105 turns into FL A1A. Drive past the park entrance station on your right, then continue to the north beach parking area. GPS trailhead coordinates: 30.458556, -81.413806

The Hike

Little Talbot Island is one of the largest undeveloped barrier islands in Florida and is part of the greater Sea Islands. The vast St. Johns River forms a large estuarine system, north of which lie the Sea Islands, the set of barrier islands extending northward into Georgia and South Carolina. Long ago they were the home of the Timucuan Indians. Later, European explorers established rice and indigo plantations there. Then they were the sites of Florida's first resorts. Beyond the island beaches rose enormous live oaks draped in Spanish moss lording over rich maritime hammocks, through which this hike travels. As the islands slope back down toward the mainland, tidal creeks rise and fall among the marshes. Time and nature move slowly here.

While seemingly every segment of Florida's coastline is being developed, preserves such as this state park offer not only a chance to explore this oceanside environment in its natural state, but also a chance to see the forces of nature at work, shaping the land—a place where water endlessly breaks against the shore and where winds sculpt the vegetation. Away from the shore you can see where the ceaseless winds and tides, along with the occasional major storm, have shifted the island itself. Barrier islands are always in a state of flux. On the north end of this hike the Atlantic is cutting into high dunes, slowly moving Little Talbot Island as surely as the moon creates the tides.

If the weather's warm, make sure and bring a little bug dope for the woods and a hat and sunglasses for the beach part of the hike. After traveling through the open park entrance road, enter the relatively cool and dark world of the maritime hammock. Palms, cedar, Southern magnolia, slash pines, and the magnificent live oaks form a woodland cathedral. Yaupon and palmetto rise from the forest floor. Occasional open areas contrast with the thick woods. Although the trail surface is sand it is more stable than you think since tree fodder and forest duff help stabilize it. However, areas that receive direct sunlight will have looser, dried-out sand. Expect an undulating trail that is never level for long and offers bona fide hills with drop-offs astride the trail that will surprise.

Occasional resting benches are situated along the path. The wide trail bordered by thick woods presents an easily followable route. Continue north in the remote heart of the island. Enjoy this slice of wild Florida before turning toward the Atlantic near the north end of Little Talbot Island. Leave the hammock and wind through dune swales topped with windswept vegetation. Stay on the trail and off the fragile dunes.

Your southbound walk along the Atlantic Ocean reveals the state of natural beaches. Craggy cedars and palms have fallen into the sands. Shells will be embedded at your feet. Ocean fodder and other vegetation will be lying on the beach, very different from the contrived, sterile, raked beaches of resorts.

Depending on the tides, make your own route along the sandy shore. Eventually the state park beach-access boardwalk will come into view. Reach the boardwalk, then travel over low windswept dunes and come to the parking area, where a picnic pavilion, restrooms, and cold outdoor showers await.

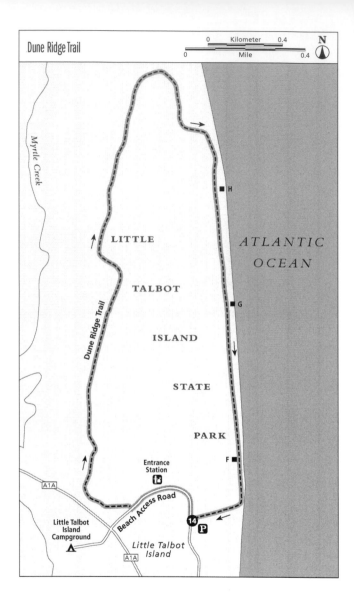

Dune Ridge Trail

Kilometer
0   0.4
Mile
0   0.4

N

Myrtle Creek

LITTLE

TALBOT

ISLAND

STATE

PARK

Dune Ridge Trail

ATLANTIC
OCEAN

H

G

F

Entrance
Station

A1A

Beach Access Road

Little Talbot
Island
Campground

14

P

Little Talbot
Island

A1A

Miles and Directions

0.0   From the north parking area near the beach, take the dedicated asphalt hike/bike path running parallel with the park entrance road back toward FL A1A.

0.2   Pass the park entrance station. Continue on the asphalt path.

0.3   Cross the park entrance road to enter full-fledged woods on a natural-surface trail. There is no parking allowed on the park entrance road at the trail's actual beginning. Pass a trailside kiosk and begin your woodland journey.

0.4   Come near FL A1A (Heckscher Drive) before turning north and running along a hilly dune line parallel with the Atlantic Ocean.

2.0   The trail curves northeasterly toward the Atlantic Ocean. Slice between big dunes as the ocean roar rises.

2.5   Reach the Atlantic Ocean in an area where dunes drop straight to the water and have been cut by the waves. Turn right (south) with the Atlantic Ocean to your left and land to your right. At high tide you may have to walk through the water a bit to get around the high dunes, which soon give way to a more-sloping beach, with ample sands for walking no matter the tides.

2.7   Pass beach marker H.

3.1   Pass beach marker G.

3.6   Pass beach marker F.

3.7   Reach the boardwalk, turn right, and cross low dunes.

3.8   Complete the hike, returning to the north parking area.

15 Fort George Island Trail

Make a loop on the grounds of an old club, now a superlative natural getaway with a sea view, hills, lush woods, and the unique opportunity to walk portions of a former golf course now being reclaimed by Mother Nature.

Distance: 3.3-mile loop
Approximate hiking time: 1.5 to 2.5 hours
Difficulty: Moderate
Trail surface: Natural surfaces
Best season: Oct through Apr
Other trail users: Bicyclists
Canine compatibility: Leashed dogs permitted

Fees and permits: No fees or permits currently required
Schedule: 8 a.m. to sunset
Maps: Fort George Island Cultural State Park, USGS Mayport
Trail contacts: Little Talbot Island State Park, 12157 Heckscher Dr., Jacksonville, FL 32226; (904) 251-2320; www .FloridaStateParks.org

Finding the trailhead: From SR 9A east of downtown, take Heckscher Drive 9.4 miles east to Fort George Road. Turn left on Fort George Road. At 0.5 mile, reach a split; stay right toward the Ribault Clubhouse. Travel a total of 1.9 miles from Heckscher Drive and reach a parking area on the far side of the road from the Ribault Club, near a historic marker indicating the site of the San Juan del Puerto Mission. GPS trailhead coordinates: 30.427786, -81.425914

The Hike

This is a great hike in a historic setting near the mouth of the St. Johns River. As with other islands of the First Coast, what came to be known as Fort George Island was once occupied by the Timucuan Indians. They got their sustenance from the nearby estuaries and left large shell mounds as evidence of their time here. When European powers set about conquering and controlling North America, the French entered these parts, and Jean Ribault claimed Fort George Island. Later, the Spaniards took over the island and established a Christian mission named San Juan del Puerto in 1587. Mission records detail life of the Timucuan, who soon succumbed to European diseases.

In the early 1700s England came to possess the island, naming it Fort George, and planned to use it as a base of operations to dislodge the Spanish from Florida. The European wranglings continued until the United States established Florida as an American territory in 1821. The island then entered its "club phase," when John Rollins established the Fort George Island Hotel in 1875, but a fire and yellow fever soon did it in.

Then, in the 1920s, the plush Ribault Club was opened. Its affluent members enjoyed a nine-hole golf course among other activities. Over time the Ribault Club lost its luster. The buildings and grounds were purchased by the state of Florida in 1989, which established Fort George Island Cultural State Park on the land. Today the refurbished Ribault Clubhouse offers an excellent meeting and retreat location, while the grounds now contain an underutilized hiking trail where you can enjoy maritime forests, as well as the unique experience of walking the holes of the old golf course. The park map shows the trail superimposed over the golf course holes.

Highlights of the hike include Point Isabel, worth the extra walk as it overlooks the Fort George River, and Mount Cornelia, one of the highest places along the Florida coast. View other nearby islands from this vantage, and finally, enjoy some vertical variation near the hike's end, when you

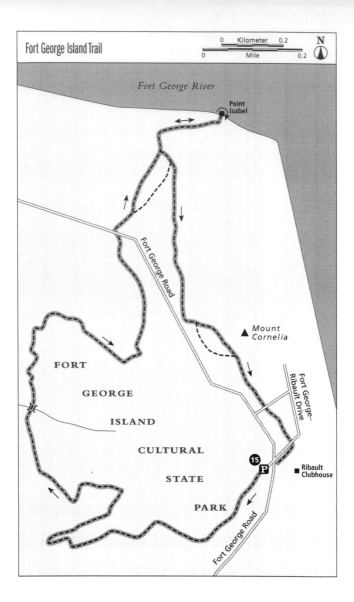

Fort George Island Trail

Fort George River

Point Isabel

Fort George Road

Mount Cornelia

FORT

GEORGE

ISLAND

CULTURAL

STATE

PARK

Fort George–Ribault Drive

15 P

Ribault Clubhouse

Fort George Road

Kilometer 0.2

Mile 0.2

N

traverse Mount Cornelia. While here, check out the nearby Kingsley Plantation with its tabby ruins and watery views.

Miles and Directions

0.0   As you face the Ribault Clubhouse, look right across a grassy field for a brown hiker sign. Walk the field toward the sign, then enter a 4-foot-wide grass and sand path in the forest. Wander between forest and clearing.

0.6   The trail curves sharply back to the northeast, then passes through a picturesque live-oak cathedral.

1.2   Span a dug canal by culvert. The forest continues to subtly change from live oak to pine and every combination of the two.

1.6   Make a sharp left near an old golf hole. The trail heads north from there.

1.9   Meet Fort George Road. Walk left about 50 feet along the road, picking up the trail on the north side of the road.

2.0   The trail splits. A shortcut heads right. Stay left, aiming for Point Isabel, crossing an open former fairway.

2.2   Take the spur trail leading straight for Point Isabel.

2.3   Reach Point Isabel. Follow concrete steps leading down to an old dock and viewing point of the Fort George River and Big Talbot Island to the north and the dunes of Little Talbot Island to the east. Note the small beach along the river's edge to your left as you look out on the river. Backtrack.

2.4   Rejoin the loop, now heading for the Ribault Clubhouse.

2.5   Keep straight past the shortcut trail intersection. Keep south amid more live oaks.

2.8   Bisect a closed sand road.

2.9   The trail splits. Keep straight, climbing over Mount Cornelia, while an easy route heads right. Note poured concrete on the path.

3.0   The easy route rejoins the main path.

3.2   Cross a park road.

3.3   Join a gravel road within sight of the Ribault Clubhouse. Turn right to return to the hiker parking area and complete the hike.

16 Castaway Island Preserve Walk

Enjoy a walk through 300 acres on the Intracoastal Waterway in an otherwise developed area of eastern Duval County near Jacksonville Beach. Castaway Island Preserve offers concrete paths and a long boardwalk, plus an observation tower, to help you explore the human and natural history of this nexus of land and sea.

Distance: 1.7 miles
Approximate hiking time: 1 to 1.5 hours
Difficulty: Easy
Trail surface: Concrete and boardwalk
Best season: Oct through Apr
Other trail users: None
Canine compatibility: Leashed dogs permitted

Fees and permits: No fees or permits required
Schedule: Sunrise to sunset
Maps: Castaway Island Preserve, USGS Jacksonville Beach
Trail contacts: Castaway Island Preserve, 2921 San Pablo Rd. South, Jacksonville FL 32224; (904) 630-4100; www.jaxparks .com

Finding the trailhead: From the Beach Boulevard exit on SR 9A east of downtown, take Beach Boulevard east for 5 miles to San Pablo Road and a traffic light. Turn left on San Pablo Road and follow it for 0.4 mile to the preserve entrance on your right. Be careful, as the entrance is hard to spot until you are right up on it. Drive a short distance into the preserve, parking just past the education center. GPS trailhead coordinates: 30.296141, -81.434185

The Hike

Castaway Island Preserve is a jewel in the city of Jacksonville's parks system—and it was about as expensive as a diamond. Situated along the west shoreline of the Intracoastal Waterway near San Pablo Creek, the 300-acre tract was the last tract of land available for park development between Atlantic and Beach Boulevards. Castaway Island was purchased in the early 2000s for over $3 million, with several hundred thousand dollars used to develop the park facilities. And to think it was once a trailer park! (At one time Navy personnel were stationed here in a small community called Pablo Palms, complete with trailers and a swimming pool.) The amenities these days focus on what nature offers—an attractive woodland enveloped by marsh and tidal creeks.

The preserve was opened back in 2004 and quickly became a favorite among locals for its access to walking trails, picnicking, or launching a canoe or kayak from a small boat basin into San Pablo Creek, part of the Intracoastal Waterway that connects to the St. Johns River. The trail system is great for kids, as it offers loads of fun interpretive information, delivered as if it were from the "survivors on Castaway Island"—critters such as raccoons and armadillos. The hike leaves the picnic area, traveling parallel to the park road before turning north to explore the interpretive nature path known as the Island Trail.

Marsh borders the land berm on which you travel, giving the walk an airy, open feel. Shorebirds may be in the nearby waters. You will certainly see them at the canoe/kayak launch if nowhere else. The Island Trail has short spurs leading to the interpretive stations. Take the elevated boardwalk extending easterly into the marsh. A labyrinth of tidal creeks snakes through the marsh grasses. These wetlands are important not only for the "survivors on Castaway Island," but also for all of Jacksonville. These wetlands help absorb waters in floods and storms but also filter pollutants from the water and provide important aquifer recharge areas. The boardwalk extends a full 0.2 mile toward Pablo Creek. A boardwalk this long is not cheap. Get your money's worth by checking out both elevated viewing areas. The Beach Boulevard Bridge arches over the Intracoastal Waterway. Houses rise on the far side of the marsh—the likely fate for this area if it were not for Preservation Project Jacksonville.

To get your full exercise value out of Castaway Island you must take every trail. This means walking the boardwalk to the canoe/kayak launch and also walking up to the covered observation tower located near the end of the main park road. Finally, pick up the concrete path leading toward San Pablo Road. This trail wanders by the picnic area, past a butterfly garden, and ends at the road next to an ancient double-trunked cedar that easily predates the state of Florida.

Miles and Directions

0.0 Pick up the concrete path in the picnic area across the park road from the education center. Begin walking east toward the Intracoastal Waterway. Cedars, palms, and wax myrtle border the trail. Turn left and join the Island Trail.

0.3 The preserve boardwalk leads right. Keep forward, walking to the Island Trail's end, which forms a small loop, then return to the boardwalk.

0.4 Begin walking the boardwalk toward San Pablo Creek and the Intracoastal Waterway. Enjoy great views of the tidal marsh from the elevated walkway.

0.6 Reach the east end of the boardwalk. Enjoy views from two elevated overlooks, then backtrack to the main park road.

0.9 After reaching the main park road, walk toward the Intracoastal Waterway and take the boardwalk leading over the water and to a canoe/kayak launch. The small basin was dug to help keep water here so paddlers could access San

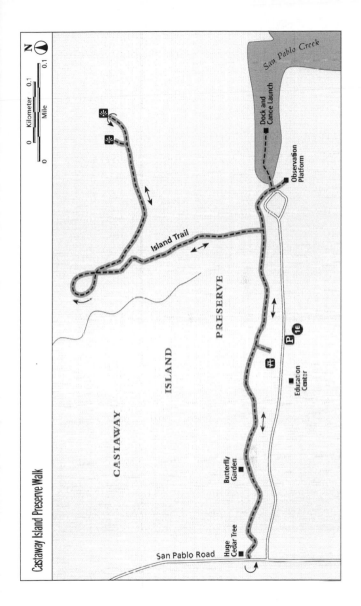

Castaway Island Preserve Walk

Pablo Creek. Also, walk up the shaded observation tower for another marsh view. Look north to spot the boardwalk you were on earlier. Now, pick up the concrete path heading toward San Pablo Road.

1.3 Pass the picnic area, trailhead, and education center, still heading toward San Pablo Road. Look for winged creatures in the butterfly garden.

1.5 Reach the park gate and San Pablo Road. Note the ancient double-trunked cedar tree. Backtrack.

1.7 Return to the trailhead and complete the hike.

17 UNF Nature Trails

This loop hike takes place on the University of North Florida campus at the Sawmill Slough Preserve. The hike uses several trails in a complex that travels through multiple habitats, including maple and cypress swamps, passing by an ancient cypress tree, and around Lake Oneida.

Distance: 3-mile loop
Approximate hiking time: 2 to 2.5 hours
Difficulty: Moderate
Trail surface: Natural surfaces and boardwalks
Best season: Oct through Apr
Other trail users: None
Canine compatibility: Dogs not allowed

Fees and permits: Parking fee required Mon through Fri; weekends and holidays are free
Schedule: Sunrise to sunset
Maps: Robert W. Loftin Nature Trails, USGS Arlington
Trail contacts: UNF Department of Recreation and Wellness, 1 UNF Dr., Jacksonville, FL 32224; (904) 620-4769; www.unf.edu /recwell

Finding the trailhead: From the University of North Florida exit east of downtown on SR 9A, take UNF Drive east for 0.5 mile to turn right into UNF parking lot 100. Immediately purchase a parking pass at the drive-through window, then park. GPS trailhead coordinates: 30.266147, -81.512056

The Hike

Back in 1973, the University of North Florida came together to build some hiking trails in the wilds of Sawmill Slough. Led by Robert Loftin, to whom the trail system is dedicated, these trails on approximately 500 acres of UNF property were opened to the public, including the very first wheelchair-accessible path in greater Jacksonville. Before the decade was out this trail system was federally recognized as a National Recreation Trail, a big acknowledgment in the trail world. Over time this trail system has been altered, expanded, and otherwise improved, including a major overhaul in 2022. The university has officially preserved this campus wildland in perpetuity, to be used for recreation, education, and research. It is also a state-protected bird sanctuary. This area deserves preservation, as it offers a variety of habitats, including open lake, hardwood swamp, pine flatwoods, sandhill forests, and seepage slopes. Today you can explore these communities using multiple trails and loops. Be apprised there is a drawback—vehicle noise from SR 9A and SR 202.

The trailhead has a fine picnic area, restrooms, and designated parking. Make sure and buy a parking pass if you are here on a weekday! The university operates nature programs for students and school groups from the area. Enrolled UNF students have the advantage of being able to check out canoes and kayaks to paddle Lake Oneida.

The university continues to improve the landscape, attempting to restore it to its natural state using prescribed fires and elimination of invasive species. The part of Sawmill Slough north of UNF Drive is off limits to visitors and is used for research purposes only. This particular hike explores the southern part of the slough and adjacent lands, starting on the preserve's longest path—the Goldenrod Trail. Exercise stations are located periodically along the path. Interpretive information enhances the trek. Pines, maples, palms, and oaks shade the trail and ground palmetto. Your hike shortly leaves left on the Big Cypress Loop. Here you can view a five-century-old bald cypress that survived the logger's ax. The reason: When you look at the tree, its trunk is divided a short ways up; that's because two trees have grown together, resulting in a wood density too tough for the saws of bygone days.

The loop continues, entering a maple swamp before curving back north and coming along a man-made lake dug for fill to elevate a nearby SR 9A interchange. The hike picks up a sandhill ridge cloaked in pines, which contrasts with Sawmill Slough, a lush hardwood swamp which you cross before meeting Lake Oneida. Circle around Lake Oneida, completing the hike. If you are looking for more trails to trek, travel the Red Maple Boardwalk as it makes a loop in wetlands near the lake.

Miles and Directions

0.0   After parking, walk toward the exit of parking lot 100. Look for the yellow blazed Goldenrod Trail leaving south from the parking area. Immediately enter rich woods on a boardwalk.

0.3   Meet the Big Cypress Loop. Veer left on this narrow single-track path. The Goldenrod Trail continues straight.

0.4   Reach a spur trail leading a short distance to a bottomland hardwood swamp and a 500-year-old bald cypress tree towering over the rest of the cypresses.

0.7   Rejoin the Goldenrod Trail on a wider track.

0.8   Reach another trail junction. Here the Goldenrod Trail makes an extra loop. Though you can keep forward and shortcut the loop, this hike stays left, going with the extra loop for maximum mileage. Circle a seasonal maple wetland centered by Buck Head Branch using a boardwalk and bridges. Come very close to noisy SR 202.

1.3   Turn right (northwest) in row-cropped pines as an unmarked trail keeps forward.

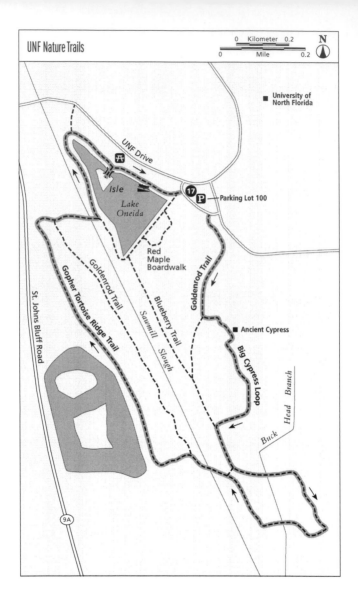

1.4 Complete the extra loop. Stay straight, still on the Goldenrod Trail.

1.5 Stay forward, joining the Gopher Tortoise Ridge Trail. Shortly come near a man-made pond, then curve north in sandy pines and turkey oaks.

2.3 Intersect the Goldenrod Trail after an easterly turn. Keep forward, rejoining the Goldenrod Trail. Cross Sawmill Slough on boardwalks.

2.4 Meet Lake Oneida and the Blueberry Trail. Turn left here and begin circling around the north arm of the lake.

2.7 A spur trail leads left to UNF Drive.

2.8 Pass a bridge leading to an island in Lake Oneida. A picnic area is nearby, too. Keep straight along the lake, passing the UNF boat rental area.

3.0 Emerge at Parking Lot 100, near the Red Maple Boardwalk, completing the hike.

18 Julington-Durbin Preserve

Enjoy a slice of nature on a preserved peninsula between Julington Creek and Durbin Creek. The alluring loop leads through regal live oak hammocks, russet pine woods, and even bottomland hardwood forests. A spur on the hike leads you to a view of Durbin Creek before returning to the trailhead.

Distance: 4.2-mile loop with spurs
Approximate hiking time: 2 to 2.5 hours
Difficulty: Moderate
Trail surface: Natural surfaces
Best season: Oct through Apr
Other trail users: Bicyclers, equestrians
Canine compatibility: Leashed dogs permitted

Fees and permits: None
Schedule: Sunrise to sunset
Maps: Julington-Durbin Preserve, USGS Bayard, Orangedale
Trail contacts: St. Johns Water Management District, 7775 Baymeadows Way, Ste. 102, Jacksonville, FL 32256; (904) 730-6270; www.sjrwmd.com

Finding the trailhead: From exit 335 on I-95 south of downtown, take Old St. Augustine Road west for 0.3 mile then turn left on Bartram Park Boulevard and follow it for 0.9 mile to the trailhead entrance on your right. Official trailhead address: 13200 Bartram Park Blvd., Jacksonville, FL 32258. GPS trailhead coordinates: 30.129319, -81.544537

The Hike

The St. Johns Water Management District has acquired and manages many properties around greater Jacksonville. Most of the parcels offer recreational opportunities from paddling to fishing to wildlife watching and of course hiking. The Julington-Durbin property, being on an undeveloped peninsula between two creeks flowing into the St. Johns River, is a jewel of a preserve, virtually encircled by development these days. Thus we can access 2,031 acres of sandhills, swamps, and picturesque flatwoods that are a delight to explore.

The St. Johns Water Management District land, bordered by these two creeks, forms 9 miles of shoreline. The long sandy ridge dividing the two creeks drops off into marshes on both sides. Despite being in an urban interface, land managers continue to safely use prescribed fire in the parcel's interior, keeping most of Julington-Durbin in a native state. A total of 9 miles of popular busy trails explore the preserve, allowing loop hikes from a little over 2 to over 6 miles. Our hike lands in the middle, a fine sampler trek that takes you through many of the ecotones found here.

Navigation here is simple. All hiker trails are color blazed. Avoid unblazed service roads. Our trek follows a white-blazed double track first in dense woods bordering a residential area before reaching pine/wiregrass sandhills giving way to live oak hammocks as well as mesic flatwoods. The white-blazed trail turns back toward the trailhead, coming within striking distance of Durbin Creek. A spur trail then drops into bottomland hardwoods. A pair of bridges leads across seasonal wetlands amidst the swamp forest to reach Durbin Creek, where you get a close-up view of this blackwater stream. Finally, return to pine-pocked sandhills before completing the trek, appreciating this piece of preserved Florida.

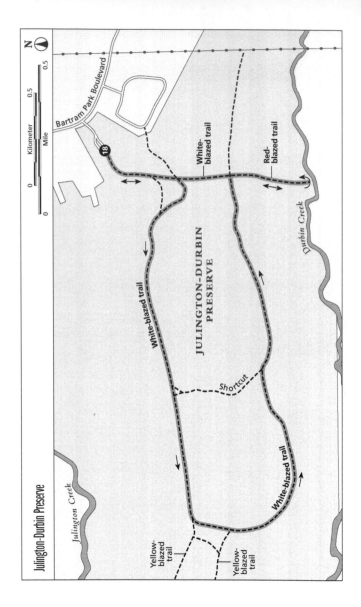

Julington-Durbin Preserve

N

Bartram Park Boulevard

18

0   Kilometer   0.5

0   Mile   0.5

White-blazed trail

Red-blazed trail

Durbin Creek

White-blazed trail

JULINGTON-DURBIN
PRESERVE

Shortcut

Julington Creek

White-blazed trail

Yellow-blazed
trail

Yellow-
blazed
trail

Miles and Directions

0.0   Leave west from the trailhead, passing picnic tables and a kiosk. Join a white-blazed doubletrack, in thick woods, not managed with prescribed fire. Ignore unblazed roads.

0.3   Reach the loop portion of the hike. Split right, turning west amidst pine and oaks, with an understory of wax myrtle and palmetto. In places the trail forms the line between fire-managed forests. Walk through pinelands and oak domes.

1.1   Pass a shortcut leading left (south) that allows for the shortest circuit hike. Keep straight with the white-blazed trail.

1.5   Come to a three-way intersection in a clearing. The yellow-blazed trail keeps straight for a long loop. We turn left (south) still on the white-blazed trail in mixed forest of pine and turkey oaks on higher ground with bay trees in the depressions.

1.7   Stay left as you pass the other end of the yellow-blazed trail. Curve east with the white-blazed trail. Enter younger pines with the trail open to the sky overhead.

2.4   Pass the other end of the shortcut trail. Stay easterly. Come near thick swamp forest to your right with sandhills to your left.

3.0   Reach an intersection. Head right (south) on the red-blazed trail. Dip to hardwood bottomland forests, crossing two bridges.

3.3   Meet coffee colored Durbin Creek in deep woods. Backtrack.

3.6   Resume the white-blazed trail, northbound, crossing pine-pocked sandhills.

3.9   Complete the loop portion of the hike. Backtrack toward the trailhead.

4.2   Arrive back at the trailhead, completing the peninsular hike.

19 Stokes Landing Conservation Area

This highlight-packed overlooked hike takes you through maritime woods adjacent to the Guana Tolomato Matanzas National Estuarine Research Reserve. The Stokes Landing tract offers a fine loop with spurs that lead to a view of the Tolomato River from Marsh Point, then to an elevated observation tower allowing distant vistas north of woods and waters. Finally, grab a final view of a tidal creek complemented with an adjacent picnic shelter at Stokes Landing.

Distance: 2.5-mile loop with spurs
Approximate hiking time: 1 to 1.5 hours
Difficulty: Moderate
Trail surface: Natural surfaces
Best season: Oct through Apr
Other trail users: Bicyclers
Canine compatibility: Leashed dogs permitted
Fees and permits: None

Schedule: Sunrise to sunset
Maps: Stokes Landing Conservation Area, USGS South Ponte Vedra Beach, Saint Augustine
Trail contacts: St. Johns Water Management District, 7775 Baymeadows Way, Ste. 102, Jacksonville, FL 32256; (904) 730-6270; www.sjrwmd.com

Finding the trailhead: From exit 323 on I-95 south of downtown Jacksonville, take International Golf Parkway east for 4.9 miles to turn right onto US 1 south. Follow it for 2 miles, then turn left onto Venetian Boulevard and follow it for 0.3 mile before turning right onto Old Dixie Drive. Follow Old Dixie for 0.1 mile, then turn left onto Lakeshore Drive and follow it for 0.7 mile to the trailhead on your left. Official trailhead address: 479 Lakeshore Dr., St. Augustine, FL 32095. GPS trailhead coordinates: 30.000000, -81.361111

The Hike

The establishment of the Guana Tolomato Matanzas National Estuarine Research Reserve indirectly led to Stokes Landing Conservation Area coming to be. Covering 76,000 acres of waters, marshes, and lands, the research reserve protects tidal terrain from Palm Coast to Ponte Vedra Beach. Stokes Landing, coming in at 286 acres, was purchased by St. Johns Water Management District as a buffer for Guana Tolomato Matanzas National Estuarine Research Reserve.

Often overlooked, Stokes Landing presents a lesser-visited hiking destination replete with distinct highlights. Using color-blazed doubletrack trails typical of St. Johns Water Management District pathways, you enter the rich maritime hardwood hammock, tracing a sometimes sloppy spur track to an overlook of the Tolomato River marshes. Next, the trek leads north through eye-pleasing varied forests of live oak, pine, palm, and cedar to an elevated observation tower, located at the margin of woodland and marshland. Here, climb the stairs and savor one of the best views in greater Jacksonville. In the near, the grasses and tidal creeks of the Tolomato River form a lynchpin, with maritime woods rising on their flanks. To the north, the narrowing waters of the Tolomato River stretch as far as the eye can see.

Your final highlight takes you to a more intimate view of an oyster bar and grass-bordered tidal stream, a tributary of Stokes Creek. A covered shelter enhances the spot and makes an ideal picnic place. From there, you complete the circuit to the trailhead, savoring the highpoints of Stokes Landing Conservation Area.

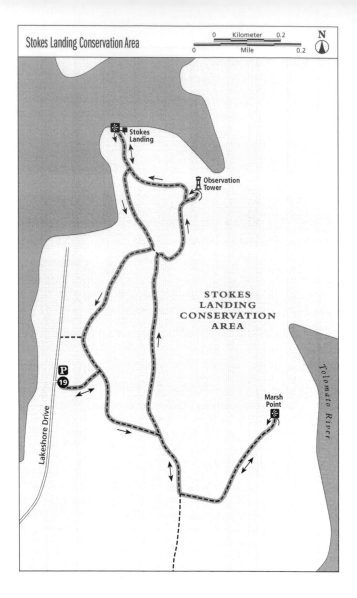

Stokes Landing Conservation Area

0   Kilometer   0.2
0   Mile   0.2

N

Stokes
Landing

Observation
Tower

STOKES
LANDING
CONSERVATION
AREA

Tolomato River

P
19

Lakeshore Drive

Marsh
Point

Miles and Directions

0.0   Join a white-blazed trail leaving from the trailhead. Work through low, potentially wet pine woods, then rise into a maritime forest dominated by live oaks.

0.1   Reach an intersection. Head right (south) with the white blazes on an inner circuit.

0.3   Stay right, joining the spur out to Marsh Point, still in primarily live oak woods with magnolia.

0.4   Make a signed left (east) toward Marsh Point as an unblazed service road keeps straight. The going ahead can be mucky in spots.

0.7   Come to Marsh Point, with an easterly view over the grasses and waters of the Tolomato River with barrier islands beyond. Backtrack to the main loop.

1.1   Resume the main loop, aka Raccoon Run Loop, heading north in live oaks and palms.

1.4   Head right at an intersection toward the observation tower in classic palm, cedar, and live oak maritime forest.

1.6   Take the short spur right, then climb the stairs up the observation tower to soak in a fine elevated view of the Tolomato River valley. Rejoin the main loop, heading northbound, then westerly.

1.8   Turn right (north) on a short spur leading to Stokes Landing and a picnic shelter. View the tidal creek in the near with waters and marsh in the distance. Return to the main loop and head south. Come along marshes to your right.

2.3   Pass a service road leading right (west) to Lakeshore Drive.

2.4   Complete the loop. Head right (west) toward the trailhead.

2.5   Arrive back at the trailhead, completing the tidal region trek.

20 GTM Reserve

Explore the heart of big Guana Tolomato Matanzas National Estuarine Research Reserve. Begin near the informative visitor center, then enter a deeply forested coastal peninsula bordered by the Tolomato and Guana Rivers. Hike near marshes as well as under pines and live oaks, then come to beautiful Shell Bluff Landing, with its small but serene white beach bordered by a shady picnic area overlooking the Tolomato River. Finally, cut back across the peninsula in woods, bridging a grassy tidal creek.

Distance: 3.2-mile loop with a spur
Approximate hiking time: 1.5 to 2 hours
Difficulty: Moderate
Trail surface: Natural surfaces
Best season: Oct through Apr
Other trail users: Bicyclers
Canine compatibility: Leashed dogs permitted

Fees and permits: Parking fee required
Schedule: Sunrise to sunset
Maps: GTM Research Reserve, USGS South Ponte Vedra Beach
Trail contacts: GTM Research Reserve, 505 Guana River Rd., Ponte Vedra Beach, FL 32082; (904) 380-8600; www.gtmnerr .org

Finding the trailhead: From exit 53 on I-295 southeast of downtown Jacksonville, take FL 202 east for 8 miles, then exit right onto US A1A and follow it south for 16.5 miles. Then turn right into the Guana Tolomato Matanzas National Estuarine Research Reserve and follow the road west past the visitor center and first parking area for a total of 0.5 mile to dead end at the main trailhead. GPS trailhead coordinates: 30.022318, -81.332621

The Hike

The Guana Tolomato Matanzas National Estuarine Research Reserve, thankfully shortened to GTM Reserve, was established in 1999, with the goal to conserve the natural and cultural resources of the Guana, Tolomato, and Matanzas Rivers, as well as to use the parcels as research and educational tools. Primarily located among tidal streams and bordering lands on a north-south axis just west of US A1A to the Florida mainland, GTM Reserve encompasses wildlife of these waterways from dolphins to manatees to shorebirds, from river otters to alligators as well as land-based critters such as deer, turkeys, and armadillos. It is truly a fascinating and very valuable reserve, and thankfully one that includes hiking trails via which we can appreciate the sights, sounds, and smells of northeast Florida among its more than 70,000 acres.

Our hike starts near the worth-a-visit visitor center for the reserve. The trails are color-coded, and the intersections are numbered with accompanying trail maps at each intersection. Spur trails to numerous relaxation benches are signed as well. You'll travel underneath a variety of forests found in the coastal Sunshine State, from live oak hammocks to high pines to maritime hardwoods as well as along tidal marshes. The walking is pleasant throughout, the highlight being Shell Bluff Landing, with its views and beach and picnic area. You'll be mostly done after leaving Shell Bluff Landing, with some more pleasant trail time that includes a bridge over a tidal creek. Still other pathways will beckon you for a return trip. Enjoy.

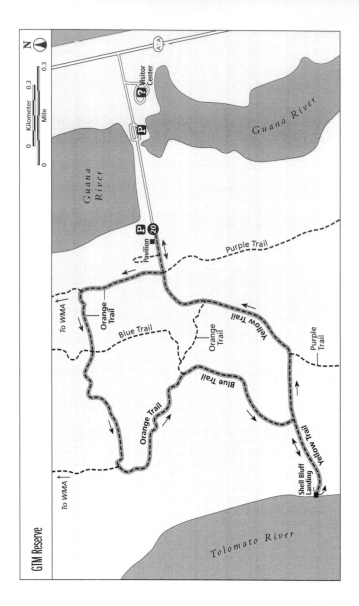

GTM Reserve

Miles and Directions

0.0   Leave west from the most westerly parking lot, joining a double-track trail under an oak archway, quickly passing a picnic shelter and restrooms with water, as well as a short all-access loop trail.

0.1   Reach a four-way intersection. Head right (north) on the Orange Trail, as the Yellow Trail, your return route, goes straight and the Purple Trail goes left. Hike under live oaks, laurel oaks, and magnolias on a wide gravel track. Look for mature pines as well.

0.4   Head left at the intersection, staying with the Orange Trail, as the track you were following keeps straight (north) for the wildlife management area (WMA) portion of the reserve. Hike west on a narrower trail amid deep shady woods. Ahead, cross a couple of elevated boardwalks over intimate, grassy estuaries.

0.6   Come to an intersection. Here, a track goes right toward the WMA, while the Blue Trail goes left. Keep straight on the Orange Trail. Wind through a low-slung maritime hammock as well as open palmetto- and gallberry-dominated locales.

1.1   Come to a trail intersection in live oaks. Head left with the Orange Trail as a track goes right into the WMA. Soon curve south, then southeasterly.

1.5   Reach yet another intersection. Here, split right with the Blue Trail, heading south. Ahead, pass a wetland on your right.

1.9   Split right on the Yellow Trail, aiming west for the Tolomato River.

2.1   Come to picturesque Shell Bluff Landing, a small quiet beach adjacent to shady forest complemented with picnic tables. Relax, then backtrack.

2.3   Return to the intersection with the Blue Trail. Stay straight with the Yellow Trail in mixed woods.

2.6   Stay left with the Yellow Trail as the long-distance Purple Trail leaves right. Come alongside a grassy marsh.

2.9   Intersect the Orange Trail. Keep straight on the Yellow Trail and shortly cross a grassy marsh on a long boardwalk bridge.

3.1   Reach the four-way intersection where you were at hike's beginning. Keep straight toward the trailhead.

3.2   Return to the trailhead, completing the walk.

THE TEN ESSENTIALS OF HIKING

American Hiking Society

Whether you plan to be gone for a couple of hours or several months, make sure to pack these items. Become familiar with these items and know how to use them.

Find other helpful resources at AmericanHiking.org/hiking-resources

1. **Appropriate Footwear**

2. **Navigation**

3. **Water** (and a way to purify it)

4. **Food**

5. **Rain Gear & Dry-Fast Layers**

6. **Safety Items** (light, fire, and a whistle)

7. **First Aid Kit**

8. **Knife or Multi-Tool**

9. **Sun Protection**

10. **Shelter**

PROTECT THE PLACES YOU LOVE TO HIKE

Become a member today and take $5 off an annual membership using the code **Falcon5**.

AmericanHiking.org/join

American Hiking Society is the only national nonprofit organization dedicated to empowering all to enjoy, share, and preserve the hiking experience.